# Federal Rules of
# Criminal Procedure

D1710704

# Federal Rules of Criminal Procedure

## As amended to December 1, 2019

Official co-publisher of NITA.
WKLegaledu.com/NITA

Address inquiries to:

Reprint Permission
National Institute for Trial Advocacy
1685 38th Street, Suite 200
Boulder, CO 80301-2735
Phone: (800) 225-6482
Fax: (720) 890-7069
E-mail: permissions@nita.org

ISBN: 978-1-60156-860-1

eISBN: 978-1-60156-861-8

FBA 1860

SUSTAINABLE
FORESTRY
INITIATIVE
Certified Chain of Custody
Promoting Sustainable Forestry
www.sfiprogram.org

Printed in the United States of America

# Contents

## TITLE III. THE GRAND JURY, THE INDICTMENT, AND THE INFORMATION

**TITLE IV. ARRAIGNMENT AND
PREPARATION FOR TRIAL**

*Contents*

Contents

## TITLE VII. POST-CONVICTION PROCEDURES

Contents

Contents

## TITLE IX. GENERAL PROVISIONS

Contents

# Contents

# TITLE I.  APPLICABILITY OF RULES

## Rule 1.  Scope; Definitions

(a) Scope.

(1) *In General.* These rules govern the procedure in all criminal proceedings in the United States district courts, the United States courts of appeals, and the Supreme Court of the United States.

(2) *State or Local Judicial Officer.* When a rule so states, it applies to a proceeding before a state or local judicial officer.

(3) *Territorial Courts.* These rules also govern the procedure in all criminal proceedings in the following courts:

(A) the district court of Guam;

(B) the district court for the Northern Mariana Islands, except as otherwise provided by law; and

(C) the district court of the Virgin Islands, except that the prosecution of offenses in that court must be by indictment or information as otherwise provided by law.

(4) *Removed Proceedings.* Although these rules govern all proceedings after removal from a state

court, state law governs a dismissal by the prosecution.

**(5)** *Excluded Proceedings.* Proceedings not governed by these rules include:

(A) the extradition and rendition of a fugitive;

(B) a civil property forfeiture for violating a federal statute;

(C) the collection of a fine or penalty;

(D) a proceeding under a statute governing juvenile delinquency to the extent the procedure is inconsistent with the statute, unless Rule 20(d) provides otherwise;

(E) a dispute between seamen under 22 U.S.C. §§ 256–258; and

(F) a proceeding against a witness in a foreign country under 28 U.S.C. § 1784.

**(b) Definitions.** The following definitions apply to these rules:

(1) "Attorney for the government" means:

(A) the Attorney General or an authorized assistant;

(B) a United States attorney or an authorized assistant;

(**C**) when applicable to cases arising under Guam law, the Guam Attorney General or other person whom Guam law authorizes to act in the matter; and

(**D**) any other attorney authorized by law to conduct proceedings under these rules as a prosecutor.

(**2**) "Court" means a federal judge performing functions authorized by law.

(**3**) "Federal judge" means:

(**A**) a justice or judge of the United States as these terms are defined in 28 U.S.C. § 451;

(**B**) a magistrate judge; and

(**C**) a judge confirmed by the United States Senate and empowered by statute in any commonwealth, territory, or possession to perform a function to which a particular rule relates.

(**4**) "Judge" means a federal judge or a state or local judicial officer.

(**5**) "Magistrate judge" means a United States magistrate judge as defined in 28 U.S.C. §§ 631–639.

(**6**) "Oath" includes an affirmation.

(**7**) "Organization" is defined in 18 U.S.C. § 18.

**(8)** "Petty offense" is defined in 18 U.S.C. § 19.

**(9)** "State" includes the District of Columbia, and any commonwealth, territory, or possession of the United States.

**(10)** "State or local judicial officer" means:

**(A)** a state or local officer authorized to act under 18 U.S.C. § 3041; and

**(B)** a judicial officer empowered by statute in the District of Columbia or in any commonwealth, territory, or possession to perform a function to which a particular rule relates.

**(11)** "Telephone" means any form of live electronic voice communication.

**(12)** "Victim" means a "crime victim" as defined in 18 U.S.C. § 3771(e).

**(c) Authority of a Justice or Judge of the United States.** When these rules authorize a magistrate judge to act, any other federal judge may also act.

## Rule 2.  Interpretation

These rules are to be interpreted to provide for the just determination of every criminal proceeding, to secure simplicity in procedure and fairness in administration, and to eliminate unjustifiable expense and delay.

# TITLE II. PRELIMINARY PROCEEDINGS

## Rule 3.  The Complaint

The complaint is a written statement of the essential facts constituting the offense charged. Except as provided in Rule 4.1, it must be made under oath before a magistrate judge or, if none is reasonably available, before a state or local judicial officer.

## Rule 4.  Arrest Warrant or Summons on a Complaint

(a) **Issuance.** If the complaint or one or more affidavits filed with the complaint establish probable cause to believe that an offense has been committed and that the defendant committed it, the judge must issue an arrest warrant to an officer authorized to execute it. At the request of an attorney for the government, the judge must issue a summons, instead of a warrant, to a person authorized to serve it. A judge may issue more than one warrant or summons on the same complaint. If an individual defendant fails to appear in response to a summons, a judge may, and upon request of an attorney for the government must, issue a warrant. If an organizational defendant fails to appear in response to a summons, a judge may take any action authorized by United States law.

(b) **Form.**

(1) *Warrant.* A warrant must:

(A) contain the defendant's name or, if it is unknown, a name or description by which the defendant can be identified with reasonable certainty;

(B) describe the offense charged in the complaint;

(C) command that the defendant be arrested and brought without unnecessary delay before a magistrate judge or, if none is reasonably available, before a state or local judicial officer; and

(D) be signed by a judge.

(2) *Summons.* A summons must be in the same form as a warrant except that it must require the defendant to appear before a magistrate judge at a stated time and place.

(c) **Execution or Service, and Return.**

(1) *By Whom.* Only a marshal or other authorized officer may execute a warrant. Any person authorized to serve a summons in a federal civil action may serve a summons.

(2) *Location.* A warrant may be executed, or a summons served, within the jurisdiction of the United States or anywhere else a federal statute authorizes an arrest. A summons to an organization

under Rule 4(c)(3)(D) may also be served at a place not within a judicial district of the United States.

(3) *Manner.*

(A) A warrant is executed by arresting the defendant. Upon arrest, an officer possessing the original or a duplicate original warrant must show it to the defendant. If the officer does not possess the warrant, the officer must inform the defendant of the warrant's existence and of the offense charged and, at the defendant's request, must show the original or a duplicate original warrant to the defendant as soon as possible.

(B) A summons is served on an individual defendant:

(i) by delivering a copy to the defendant personally; or

(ii) by leaving a copy at the defendant's residence or usual place of abode with a person of suitable age and discretion residing at that location and by mailing a copy to the defendant's last known address.

(C) A summons is served on an organization in a judicial district of the United States by delivering a copy to an officer, to a managing or general agent, or to another agent appointed or legally authorized to receive service of process. If the agent is one authorized by statute and the statute so requires, a copy must also be mailed to the organization.

**(D)** A summons is served on an organization not within a judicial district of the United States:

(i)   by delivering a copy, in a manner authorized by the foreign jurisdiction's law, to an officer, to a managing or general agent, or to an agent appointed or legally authorized to receive service of process; or

(ii)  by any other means that gives notice, including one that is:

(a)  stipulated by the parties;

(b)  undertaken by a foreign authority in response to a letter rogatory, a letter of request, or a request submitted under an applicable international agreement; or

(c)  permitted by an applicable international agreement.

(4) *Return.*

**(A)** After executing a warrant, the officer must return it to the judge before whom the defendant is brought in accordance with Rule 5. The officer may do so by reliable electronic means. At the request of an attorney for the government, an unexecuted warrant must be brought back to and canceled by a magistrate judge or, if none is reasonably available, by a state or local judicial officer.

**(B)** The person to whom a summons was delivered for service must return it on or before the return day.

**(C)** At the request of an attorney for the government, a judge may deliver an unexecuted warrant, an unserved summons, or a copy of the warrant or summons to the marshal or other authorized person for execution or service.

**(d)** **Warrant by Telephone or Other Reliable Electronic Means.** In accordance with Rule 4.1, a magistrate judge may issue a warrant or summons based on the information communicated by telephone or other reliable electronic means.

## Rule 4.1. Complaint, Warrant, or Summons by Telephone or Other Reliable Electronic Means

**(a)** **In General.** A magistrate judge may consider information communicated by telephone or other reliable means when deciding whether to approve a complaint or to issue a warrant or summons.

(b) **Procedures.** If a magistrate judge decides to proceed under this rule, the following procedures apply:

(1) *Taking Testimony Under Oath.* The judge must place under oath—and may examine—the applicant and any person on whose testimony the application is based.

(2) *Creating a Record of the Testimony and Exhibits.*

(A) Testimony Limited to Attestation. If the applicant does no more than attest to the contents of a written affidavit submitted by reliable electronic means, the judge must acknowledge the attestation in writing on the affidavit.

(B) Additional Testimony or Exhibits. If the judge considers additional testimony or exhibits, the judge must:

(i) have the testimony recorded verbatim by an electronic recording device, by a court reporter, or in writing;

(ii) have any recording or reporter's notes transcribed, have the transcription certified as accurate, and file it;

(iii) sign any other written record, certify its accuracy, and file it; and

(iv) make sure that the exhibits are filed.

**(3)** *Preparing a Proposed Duplicate Original of a Complaint, Warrant, or Summons.* The applicant must prepare a proposed duplicate original of a complaint, warrant, or summons, and must read or otherwise transmit its contents verbatim to the judge.

**(4)** *Preparing an Original Complaint, Warrant, or Summons.* If the applicant reads the contents of the proposed duplicate original, the judge must enter those contents into an original complaint, warrant, or summons. If the applicant transmits the contents by reliable electronic means, the transmission received by the judge may serve as the original.

**(5)** *Modification.* The judge may modify the complaint, warrant, or summons. The judge must then:

    **(A)** transmit the modified version to the applicant by reliable electronic means; or

    **(B)** file the modified original and direct the applicant to modify the proposed duplicate original accordingly.

**(6)** *Issuance.* To issue the warrant or summons, the judge must:

    **(A)** sign the original documents;

    **(B)** enter the date and time of issuance on the warrant or summons; and

(C) transmit the warrant or summons by reliable electronic means to the applicant or direct the applicant to sign the judge's name and enter the date and time on the duplicate original.

(c) **Suppression Limited.** Absent a finding of bad faith, evidence obtained from a warrant issued under this rule is not subject to suppression on the ground that issuing the warrant in this manner was unreasonable under the circumstances.

## Rule 5.  Initial Appearance

(a) **In General.**

(1) *Appearance Upon an Arrest.*

(A) A person making an arrest within the United States must take the defendant without unnecessary delay before a magistrate judge, or before a state or local judicial officer as Rule 5(c) provides, unless a statute provides otherwise.

(B) A person making an arrest outside the United States must take the defendant without unnecessary delay before a magistrate judge, unless a statute provides otherwise.

(2) *Exceptions.*

(A) An officer making an arrest under a warrant issued upon a complaint charging solely a violation of 18 U.S.C. § 1073 need not comply with this rule if:

(i) the person arrested is transferred without unnecessary delay to the custody of appropriate state or local authorities in the district of arrest; and

(ii) an attorney for the government moves promptly, in the district where the warrant was issued, to dismiss the complaint.

**(B)** If a defendant is arrested for violating probation or supervised release, Rule 32.1 applies.

**(C)** If a defendant is arrested for failing to appear in another district, Rule 40 applies.

**(3)** *Appearance Upon a Summons.* When a defendant appears in response to a summons under Rule 4, a magistrate judge must proceed under Rule 5(d) or (e), as applicable.

**(b) Arrest Without a Warrant.** If a defendant is arrested without a warrant, a complaint meeting Rule 4(a)'s requirement of probable cause must be promptly filed in the district where the offense was allegedly committed.

**(c) Place of Initial Appearance; Transfer to Another District.**

**(1)** *Arrest in the District Where the Offense Was Allegedly Committed.* If the defendant is arrested in the district where the offense was allegedly committed:

**(A)** the initial appearance must be in that district; and

**(B)** if a magistrate judge is not reasonably available, the initial appearance may be before a state or local judicial officer.

**(2)** *Arrest in a District Other Than Where the Offense Was Allegedly Committed.* If the defendant was arrested in a district other than where the offense was allegedly committed, the initial appearance must be:

**(A)** in the district of arrest; or

**(B)** in an adjacent district if:

**(i)** the appearance can occur more promptly there; or

**(ii)** the offense was allegedly committed there and the initial appearance will occur on the day of arrest.

**(3)** *Procedures in a District Other Than Where the Offense Was Allegedly Committed.* If the initial appearance occurs in a district other than where the offense was allegedly committed, the following procedures apply:

**(A)** the magistrate judge must inform the defendant about the provisions of Rule 20;

**(B)** if the defendant was arrested without a warrant, the district court where the offense was allegedly committed must first issue a warrant before the magistrate judge transfers the defendant to that district;

**(C)** the magistrate judge must conduct a preliminary hearing if required by Rule 5.1;

**(D)** the magistrate judge must transfer the defendant to the district where the offense was allegedly committed if:

   **(i)** the government produces the warrant, a certified copy of the warrant, or a reliable electronic form of either; and

   **(ii)** the judge finds that the defendant is the same person named in the indictment, information, or warrant; and

**(E)** when a defendant is transferred and discharged, the clerk must promptly transmit the papers and any bail to the clerk in the district where the offense was allegedly committed.

**(4)** *Procedure for Persons Extradited to the United States.* If the defendant is surrendered to the United States in accordance with a request for the defendant's extradition, the initial appearance must be in the district (or one of the districts) where the offense is charged.

## (d) Procedure in a Felony Case.

(1) *Advice.* If the defendant is charged with a felony, the judge must inform the defendant of the following:

(A) the complaint against the defendant, and any affidavit filed with it;

(B) the defendant's right to retain counsel or to request that counsel be appointed if the defendant cannot obtain counsel;

(C) the circumstances, if any, under which the defendant may secure pretrial release;

(D) any right to a preliminary hearing;

(E) the defendant's right not to make a statement, and that any statement made may be used against the defendant; and

(F) that a defendant who is not a United States citizen may request that an attorney for the government or a federal law enforcement official notify a consular officer from the defendant's country of nationality that the defendant has been arrested—but that even without the defendant's request, a treaty or other international agreement may require consular notification.

(2) *Consulting with Counsel.* The judge must allow the defendant reasonable opportunity to consult with counsel.

(3) *Detention or Release.* The judge must detain or release the defendant as provided by statute or these rules.

(4) *Plea.* A defendant may be asked to plead only under Rule 10.

(e) **Procedure in a Misdemeanor Case.** If the defendant is charged with a misdemeanor only, the judge must inform the defendant in accordance with Rule 58(b)(2).

(f) **Video Teleconferencing.** Video teleconferencing may be used to conduct an appearance under this rule if the defendant consents.

## Rule 5.1. Preliminary Hearing

(a) **In General.** If a defendant is charged with an offense other than a petty offense, a magistrate judge must conduct a preliminary hearing unless:

(1) the defendant waives the hearing;

(2) the defendant is indicted;

(3) the government files an information under Rule 7(b) charging the defendant with a felony;

(4) the government files an information charging the defendant with a misdemeanor; or

(5) the defendant is charged with a misdemeanor and consents to trial before a magistrate judge.

(b) **Selecting a District.** A defendant arrested in a district other than where the offense was allegedly committed may elect to have the preliminary hearing conducted in the district where the prosecution is pending.

(c) **Scheduling.** The magistrate judge must hold the preliminary hearing within a reasonable time, but no later than 14 days after the initial appearance if the defendant is in custody and no later than 21 days if not in custody.

(d) **Extending the Time.** With the defendant's consent and upon a showing of good cause—taking into account the public interest in the prompt disposition of criminal cases—a magistrate judge may extend the time limits in Rule 5.1(c) one or more times. If the defendant does not consent, the magistrate judge may extend the time limits only on a showing that extraordinary circumstances exist and justice requires the delay.

(e) **Hearing and Finding.** At the preliminary hearing, the defendant may cross-examine adverse witnesses and may introduce evidence but may not object to evidence on the ground that it was unlawfully acquired. If the magistrate judge finds probable cause to believe an offense has been committed and the defendant committed it, the magistrate judge must promptly require the defendant to appear for further proceedings.

**(f) Discharging the Defendant.** If the magistrate judge finds no probable cause to believe an offense has been committed or the defendant committed it, the magistrate judge must dismiss the complaint and discharge the defendant. A discharge does not preclude the government from later prosecuting the defendant for the same offense.

**(g) Recording the Proceedings.** The preliminary hearing must be recorded by a court reporter or by a suitable recording device. A recording of the proceeding may be made available to any party upon request. A copy of the recording and a transcript may be provided to any party upon request and upon any payment required by applicable Judicial Conference regulations.

**(h) Producing a Statement.**

(1) *In General.* Rule 26.2(a)–(d) and (f) applies at any hearing under this rule, unless the magistrate judge for good cause rules otherwise in a particular case.

(2) *Sanctions for Not Producing a Statement.*
If a party disobeys a Rule 26.2 order to deliver
a statement to the moving party, the magistrate
judge must not consider the testimony of a witness
whose statement is withheld.

# TITLE III.   THE GRAND JURY, THE INDICTMENT, AND THE INFORMATION

## Rule 6.   The Grand Jury

(a) **Summoning a Grand Jury.**

(1) *In General.* When the public interest so requires, the court must order that one or more grand juries be summoned. A grand jury must have 16 to 23 members, and the court must order that enough legally qualified persons be summoned to meet this requirement.

(2) *Alternate Jurors.* When a grand jury is selected, the court may also select alternate jurors. Alternate jurors must have the same qualifications and be selected in the same manner as any other juror. Alternate jurors replace jurors in the same sequence in which the alternates were selected. An alternate juror who replaces a juror is subject to the same challenges, takes the same oath, and has the same authority as the other jurors.

(b) **Objection to the Grand Jury or to a Grand Juror.**

(1) *Challenges.* Either the government or a defendant may challenge the grand jury on the ground that it was not lawfully drawn, summoned, or

selected, and may challenge an individual juror on the ground that the juror is not legally qualified.

**(2)** *Motion to Dismiss an Indictment.* A party may move to dismiss the indictment based on an objection to the grand jury or on an individual juror's lack of legal qualification, unless the court has previously ruled on the same objection under Rule 6(b)(1). The motion to dismiss is governed by 28 U.S.C. § 1867(e). The court must not dismiss the indictment on the ground that a grand juror was not legally qualified if the record shows that at least 12 qualified jurors concurred in the indictment.

**(c) Foreperson and Deputy Foreperson.** The court will appoint one juror as the foreperson and another as the deputy foreperson. In the foreperson's absence, the deputy foreperson will act as the foreperson. The foreperson may administer oaths and affirmations and will sign all indictments. The foreperson—or another juror designated by the foreperson—will record the number of jurors concurring in every indictment and will file the record with the clerk, but the record may not be made public unless the court so orders.

**(d) Who May Be Present.**

**(1)** *While the Grand Jury Is in Session.* The following persons may be present while the grand jury is in session: attorneys for the government, the witness being questioned, interpreters when needed, and a court reporter or an operator of a recording device.

**(2)** *During Deliberations and Voting.* No person other than the jurors, and any interpreter needed to assist a hearing-impaired or speech-impaired juror, may be present while the grand jury is deliberating or voting.

**(e) Recording and Disclosing the Proceedings.**

**(1)** *Recording the Proceedings.* Except while the grand jury is deliberating or voting, all proceedings must be recorded by a court reporter or by a suitable recording device. But the validity of a prosecution is not affected by the unintentional failure to make a recording. Unless the court orders otherwise, an attorney for the government will retain control of the recording, the reporter's notes, and any transcript prepared from those notes.

**(2)** *Secrecy.*

**(A)** No obligation of secrecy may be imposed on any person except in accordance with Rule 6(e) (2)(B).

(**B**) Unless these rules provide otherwise, the following persons must not disclose a matter occurring before the grand jury:

(i) a grand juror;

(ii) an interpreter;

(iii) a court reporter;

(iv) an operator of a recording device;

(v) a person who transcribes recorded testimony;

(vi) an attorney for the government; or

(vii) a person to whom disclosure is made under Rule 6(e)(3)(A)(ii) or (iii).

(3) *Exceptions.*

(**A**) Disclosure of a grand-jury matter—other than the grand jury's deliberations or any grand juror's vote—may be made to:

(i) an attorney for the government for use in performing that attorney's duty;

(ii) any government personnel—including those of a state, state subdivision, Indian tribe, or foreign government—that an attorney for the government considers necessary to assist in performing that attorney's duty to enforce federal criminal law; or

(iii) a person authorized by 18 U.S.C. § 3322.

**(B)** A person to whom information is disclosed under Rule 6(e)(3)(A)(ii) may use that information only to assist an attorney for the government in performing that attorney's duty to enforce federal criminal law. An attorney for the government must promptly provide the court that impaneled the grand jury with the names of all persons to whom a disclosure has been made, and must certify that the attorney has advised those persons of their obligation of secrecy under this rule.

**(C)** An attorney for the government may disclose any grand-jury matter to another federal grand jury.

**(D)** An attorney for the government may disclose any grand-jury matter involving foreign intelligence, counterintelligence (as defined in 50 U.S.C. § 3003), or foreign intelligence information (as defined in Rule 6(e)(3)(D)(iii)) to any federal law enforcement, intelligence, protective, immigration, national defense, or national security official to assist the official receiving the information in the performance of that official's duties. An attorney for the government may also disclose any grand-jury matter involving, within the United States or elsewhere, a threat of attack or other grave hostile acts of a foreign power or its agent, a threat of domestic or international sabotage or terrorism, or clandestine intelligence gathering activities by an intelligence service or network of a foreign power or by its agent, to any appropriate federal, state, state subdivision, Indian tribal, or foreign government official, for the purpose of preventing or responding to such threat or activities.

(i) Any official who receives information under Rule 6(e)(3)(D) may use the information only as necessary in the conduct of that person's official duties subject to any limitations on the unauthorized disclosure of such information. Any state, state subdivision, Indian tribal, or foreign government official who receives information under Rule 6(e)(3)(D) may use the information only in a manner consistent with any guidelines issued by the Attorney General and the Director of National Intelligence.

(ii) Within a reasonable time after disclosure is made under Rule 6(e)(3)(D), an attorney for the government must file, under seal, a notice with the court in the district where the grand jury convened stating that such information was disclosed and the departments, agencies, or entities to which the disclosure was made.

(iii) As used in Rule 6(e)(3)(D), the term "foreign intelligence information" means:

(a) information, whether or not it concerns a United States person, that relates to the ability of the United States to protect against—

- actual or potential attack or other grave hostile acts of a foreign power or its agent;

- sabotage or international terrorism by a foreign power or its agent; or

- clandestine intelligence activities by an intelligence service or network of a foreign power or by its agent; or

(b) information, whether or not it concerns a United States person, with respect to a foreign power or foreign territory that relates to—

- the national defense or the security of the United States; or

- the conduct of the foreign affairs of the United States.

**(E)** The court may authorize disclosure—at a time, in a manner, and subject to any other conditions that it directs—of a grand-jury matter:

**(i)** preliminarily to or in connection with a judicial proceeding;

**(ii)** at the request of a defendant who shows that a ground may exist to dismiss the indictment because of a matter that occurred before the grand jury;

**(iii)** at the request of the government, when sought by a foreign court or prosecutor for use in an official criminal investigation;

**(iv)** at the request of the government if it shows that the matter may disclose a violation of State, Indian tribal, or foreign criminal law, as long as the disclosure is to an appropriate state, state-subdivision, Indian tribal, or foreign government official for the purpose of enforcing that law; or

**(v)** at the request of the government if it shows that the matter may disclose a violation of military criminal law under the Uniform Code of Military Justice, as long as the disclosure is to an appropriate military official for the purpose of enforcing that law.

**(F)** A petition to disclose a grand-jury matter under Rule 6(e)(3)(E)(i) must be filed in the district where the grand jury convened. Unless the hearing is ex parte—as it may be when the government is the petitioner—the petitioner must serve the petition on, and the court must afford a reasonable opportunity to appear and be heard to:

(i) an attorney for the government;

(ii) the parties to the judicial proceeding; and

(iii) any other person whom the court may designate.

**(G)** If the petition to disclose arises out of a judicial proceeding in another district, the petitioned court must transfer the petition to the other court unless the petitioned court can reasonably determine whether disclosure is proper. If the petitioned court decides to transfer, it must send to the transferee court the material sought to be disclosed, if feasible, and a written evaluation of the need for continued grand jury secrecy. The transferee court must afford those persons identified in Rule 6(e)(3)(F) a reasonable opportunity to appear and be heard.

**(4)** *Sealed Indictment.* The magistrate judge to whom an indictment is returned may direct that the indictment be kept secret until the defendant is in custody or has been released pending trial. The clerk must then seal the indictment, and no person may disclose the indictment's existence except as necessary to issue or execute a warrant or summons.

(5) *Closed Hearing.* Subject to any right to an open hearing in a contempt proceeding, the court must close any hearing to the extent necessary to prevent disclosure of a matter occurring before a grand jury.

(6) *Sealed Records.* Records, orders, and subpoenas relating to grand-jury proceedings must be kept under seal to the extent and as long as necessary to prevent the unauthorized disclosure of a matter occurring before a grand jury.

(7) *Contempt.* A knowing violation of Rule 6, or of any guidelines jointly issued by the Attorney General and the Director of National Intelligence under Rule 6, may be punished as a contempt of court.

(f) **Indictment and Return.** A grand jury may indict only if at least 12 jurors concur. The grand jury—or its foreperson or deputy foreperson—must return the indictment to a magistrate judge in open court. To avoid unnecessary cost or delay, the magistrate judge may take the return by video teleconference from the court where the grand jury sits. If a complaint or information is pending against the defendant and 12 jurors do not concur in the indictment, the foreperson must promptly and in writing report the lack of concurrence to the magistrate judge.

**(g) Discharging the Grand Jury.** A grand jury must serve until the court discharges it, but it may serve more than 18 months only if the court, having determined that an extension is in the public interest, extends the grand jury's service. An extension may be granted for no more than 6 months, except as otherwise provided by statute.

**(h) Excusing a Juror.** At any time, for good cause, the court may excuse a juror either temporarily or permanently, and if permanently, the court may impanel an alternate juror in place of the excused juror.

**(i) "Indian Tribe" Defined.** "Indian tribe" means an Indian tribe recognized by the Secretary of the Interior on a list published in the Federal Register under 25 U.S.C. § 479a-1.

## Rule 7.  The Indictment and the Information

(a) **When Used.**

(1) *Felony.* An offense (other than criminal contempt) must be prosecuted by an indictment if it is punishable:

**(A)** by death; or

**(B)** by imprisonment for more than one year.

**(2)** *Misdemeanor.* An offense punishable by imprisonment for one year or less may be prosecuted in accordance with Rule 58(b)(1).

**(b) Waiving Indictment.** An offense punishable by imprisonment for more than one year may be prosecuted by information if the defendant—in open court and after being advised of the nature of the charge and of the defendant's rights—waives prosecution by indictment.

**(c) Nature and Contents.**

**(1)** *In General.* The indictment or information must be a plain, concise, and definite written statement of the essential facts constituting the offense charged and must be signed by an attorney for the government. It need not contain a formal introduction or conclusion. A count may incorporate by reference an allegation made in another count. A count may allege that the means by which the defendant committed the offense are unknown or that the defendant committed it by one or more specified means. For each count, the indictment or information must give the official or customary citation of the statute, rule, regulation, or other provision of law that the defendant is alleged to have violated. For purposes of an indictment referred to in section 3282 of title 18, United States Code, for which the identity of the defendant is unknown, it shall be sufficient for the indictment to describe the defendant as an individual whose name is unknown, but who has a particular DNA profile, as that term is defined in section 3282.

(2) *Citation Error.* Unless the defendant was misled and thereby prejudiced, neither an error in a citation nor a citation's omission is a ground to dismiss the indictment or information or to reverse a conviction.

(d) **Surplusage.** Upon the defendant's motion, the court may strike surplusage from the indictment or information.

(e) **Amending an Information.** Unless an additional or different offense is charged or a substantial right of the defendant is prejudiced, the court may permit an information to be amended at any time before the verdict or finding.

(f) **Bill of Particulars.** The court may direct the government to file a bill of particulars. The defendant may move for a bill of particulars before or within 14 days after arraignment or at a later time if the court permits. The government may amend a bill of particulars subject to such conditions as justice requires.

## Rule 8. Joinder of Offenses or Defendants

(a) **Joinder of Offenses.** The indictment or information may charge a defendant in separate counts with 2 or more offenses if the offenses charged—whether felonies or misdemeanors or both—are of the same or similar character, or are based on the same act or transaction, or are connected with or constitute parts of a common scheme or plan.

(b) **Joinder of Defendants.** The indictment or information may charge 2 or more defendants if they are alleged to have participated in the same act or transaction, or in the same series of acts or transactions, constituting an offense or offenses. The defendants may be charged in one or more counts together or separately. All defendants need not be charged in each count.

## Rule 9. Arrest Warrant or Summons on an Indictment or Information

(a) **Issuance.** The court must issue a warrant—or at the government's request, a summons—for each defendant named in an indictment or named in an information if one or more affidavits accompanying the information establish probable cause to believe that an offense has been committed and that the defendant committed it. The court may issue more than one warrant or summons for the same defendant. If a defendant fails to appear in response to a summons, the court may, and upon request of an attorney for the government must, issue a warrant. The court must issue the arrest warrant to an officer authorized to execute it or the summons to a person authorized to serve it.

(b) **Form.**

(1) *Warrant.* The warrant must conform to Rule 4(b)(1) except that it must be signed by the clerk and must describe the offense charged in the indictment or information.

(2) *Summons.* The summons must be in the same form as a warrant except that it must require the defendant to appear before the court at a stated time and place.

(c) **Execution or Service; Return; Initial Appearance.**

(1) *Execution or Service.*

(A) The warrant must be executed or the summons served as provided in Rule 4(c)(1), (2), and (3).

(B) The officer executing the warrant must proceed in accordance with Rule 5(a)(1).

(2) *Return.* A warrant or summons must be returned in accordance with Rule 4(c)(4).

(3) *Initial Appearance.* When an arrested or summoned defendant first appears before the court, the judge must proceed under Rule 5.

(d) **Warrant by Telephone or Other Means.** In accordance with Rule 4.1, a magistrate judge may issue an arrest warrant or summons based on information communicated by telephone or other reliable electronic means.

# TITLE IV.  ARRAIGNMENT AND PREPARATION FOR TRIAL

## Rule 10.  Arraignment

(a) **In General.** An arraignment must be conducted in open court and must consist of:

(1) ensuring that the defendant has a copy of the indictment or information;

(2) reading the indictment or information to the defendant or stating to the defendant the substance of the charge; and then

(3) asking the defendant to plead to the indictment or information.

(b) **Waiving Appearance.** A defendant need not be present for the arraignment if:

(1) the defendant has been charged by indictment or misdemeanor information;

(2) the defendant, in a written waiver signed by both the defendant and defense counsel, has waived appearance and has affirmed that the defendant received a copy of the indictment or information and that the plea is not guilty; and

(3) the court accepts the waiver.

(c) **Video Teleconferencing.** Video teleconferencing may be used to arraign a defendant if the defendant consents.

# Rule 11. Pleas

(a) **Entering a Plea.**

(1) *In General.* A defendant may plead not guilty, guilty, or (with the court's consent) nolo contendere.

(2) *Conditional Plea.* With the consent of the court and the government, a defendant may enter a conditional plea of guilty or nolo contendere, reserving in writing the right to have an appellate court review an adverse determination of a specified pretrial motion. A defendant who prevails on appeal may then withdraw the plea.

(3) *Nolo Contendere Plea.* Before accepting a plea of nolo contendere, the court must consider the parties' views and the public interest in the effective administration of justice.

(4) *Failure to Enter a Plea.* If a defendant refuses to enter a plea or if a defendant organization fails to appear, the court must enter a plea of not guilty.

(b) **Considering and Accepting a Guilty or Nolo Contendere Plea.**

(1) *Advising and Questioning the Defendant.* Before the court accepts a plea of guilty or nolo contendere, the defendant may be placed under oath, and the court must address the defendant personally in open court. During this address,

the court must inform the defendant of, and determine that the defendant understands, the following:

(A) the government's right, in a prosecution for perjury or false statement, to use against the defendant any statement that the defendant gives under oath;

(B) the right to plead not guilty, or having already so pleaded, to persist in that plea;

(C) the right to a jury trial;

(D) the right to be represented by counsel—and if necessary have the court appoint counsel—at trial and at every other stage of the proceeding;

(E) the right at trial to confront and cross-examine adverse witnesses, to be protected from compelled self-incrimination, to testify and present evidence, and to compel the attendance of witnesses;

(F) the defendant's waiver of these trial rights if the court accepts a plea of guilty or nolo contendere;

(G) the nature of each charge to which the defendant is pleading;

(**H**) any maximum possible penalty, including imprisonment, fine, and term of supervised release;

(**I**) any mandatory minimum penalty;

(**J**) any applicable forfeiture;

(**K**) the court's authority to order restitution;

(**L**) the court's obligation to impose a special assessment;

(**M**) in determining a sentence, the court's obligation to calculate the applicable sentencing-guideline range and to consider that range, possible departures under the Sentencing Guidelines, and other sentencing factors under 18 U.S.C. § 3553(a);

(**N**) the terms of any plea-agreement provision waiving the right to appeal or to collaterally attack the sentence; and

(**O**) that, if convicted, a defendant who is not a United States citizen may be removed from the United States, denied citizenship, and denied admission to the United States in the future.

(2) *Ensuring That a Plea Is Voluntary.* Before accepting a plea of guilty or nolo contendere, the court must address the defendant personally in open court and determine that the plea is voluntary

and did not result from force, threats, or promises (other than promises in a plea agreement).

**(3)** *Determining the Factual Basis for a Plea.* Before entering judgment on a guilty plea, the court must determine that there is a factual basis for the plea.

**(c)** **Plea Agreement Procedure.**

**(1)** *In General.* An attorney for the government and the defendant's attorney, or the defendant when proceeding pro se, may discuss and reach a plea agreement. The court must not participate in these discussions. If the defendant pleads guilty or nolo contendere to either a charged offense or a lesser or related offense, the plea agreement may specify that an attorney for the government will:

**(A)** not bring, or will move to dismiss, other charges;

**(B)** recommend, or agree not to oppose the defendant's request, that a particular sentence or sentencing range is appropriate or that a particular provision of the Sentencing Guidelines, or policy statement, or sentencing factor does or does not apply (such a recommendation or request does not bind the court); or

(**C**) agree that a specific sentence or sentencing range is the appropriate disposition of the case, or that a particular provision of the Sentencing Guidelines, or policy statement, or sentencing factor does or does not apply (such a recommendation or request binds the court once the court accepts the plea agreement).

(**2**) *Disclosing a Plea Agreement.* The parties must disclose the plea agreement in open court when the plea is offered, unless the court for good cause allows the parties to disclose the plea agreement in camera.

(**3**) *Judicial Consideration of a Plea Agreement.*

(**A**) To the extent the plea agreement is of the type specified in Rule 11(c)(1)(A) or (C), the court may accept the agreement, reject it, or defer a decision until the court has reviewed the presentence report.

(**B**) To the extent the plea agreement is of the type specified in Rule 11(c)(1)(B), the court must advise the defendant that the defendant has no right to withdraw the plea if the court does not follow the recommendation or request.

(**4**) *Accepting a Plea Agreement.* If the court accepts the plea agreement, it must inform the defendant that to the extent the plea agreement is of the type specified in Rule 11(c)(1)(A) or (C), the agreed disposition will be included in the judgment.

**(5)** *Rejecting a Plea Agreement.* If the court rejects a plea agreement containing provisions of the type specified in Rule 11(c)(1)(A) or (C), the court must do the following on the record and in open court (or, for good cause, in camera):

    **(A)** inform the parties that the court rejects the plea agreement;

    **(B)** advise the defendant personally that the court is not required to follow the plea agreement and give the defendant an opportunity to withdraw the plea; and

    **(C)** advise the defendant personally that if the plea is not withdrawn, the court may dispose of the case less favorably toward the defendant than the plea agreement contemplated.

**(d) Withdrawing a Guilty or Nolo Contendere Plea.** A defendant may withdraw a plea of guilty or nolo contendere:

    **(1)** before the court accepts the plea, for any reason or no reason; or

    **(2)** after the court accepts the plea, but before it imposes sentence if:

(A) the court rejects a plea agreement under Rule 11(c)(5); or

(B) the defendant can show a fair and just reason for requesting the withdrawal.

(e) **Finality of a Guilty or Nolo Contendere Plea.** After the court imposes sentence, the defendant may not withdraw a plea of guilty or nolo contendere, and the plea may be set aside only on direct appeal or collateral attack.

(f) **Admissibility or Inadmissibility of a Plea, Plea Discussions, and Related Statements.** The admissibility or inadmissibility of a plea, a plea discussion, and any related statement is governed by Federal Rule of Evidence 410.

(g) **Recording the Proceedings.** The proceedings during which the defendant enters a plea must be recorded by a court reporter or by a suitable recording device. If there is a guilty plea or a nolo contendere plea, the record must include the inquiries and advice to the defendant required under Rule 11(b) and (c).

(h) **Harmless Error.** A variance from the requirements of this rule is harmless error if it does not affect substantial rights.

## Rule 12. Pleadings and Pretrial Motions

**(a) Pleadings.** The pleadings in a criminal proceeding are the indictment, the information, and the pleas of not guilty, guilty, and nolo contendere.

**(b) Pretrial Motions.**

(1) *In General.* A party may raise by pretrial motion any defense, objection, or request that the court can determine without a trial on the merits. Rule 47 applies to a pretrial motion.

(2) *Motions That May Be Made at Any Time.* A motion that the court lacks jurisdiction may be made at any time while the case is pending.

(3) *Motions That Must Be Made Before Trial.* The following defenses, objections, and requests must be raised by pretrial motion if the basis for the motion is then reasonably available and the motion can be determined without a trial on the merits:

(A) a defect in instituting the prosecution, including:

(i) improper venue;

(ii) preindictment delay;

(iii) a violation of the constitutional right to a speedy trial;

(iv) selective or vindictive prosecution; and

(v) an error in the grand-jury proceeding or preliminary hearing;

(B) a defect in the indictment or information, including:

(i) joining two or more offenses in the same count (duplicity);

(ii) charging the same offense in more than one count (multiplicity);

(iii) lack of specificity;

(iv) improper joinder; and

(v) failure to state an offense;

(C) suppression of evidence;

(D) severance of charges or defendants under Rule 14; and

(E) discovery under Rule 16.

(4) *Notice of the Government's Intent to Use Evidence.*

(A) *At the Government's Discretion.* At the arraignment or as soon afterward as practicable, the government may notify the defendant of its intent to use specified evidence at trial in order to afford the defendant an opportunity to object before trial under Rule 12(b)(3)(C).

(B) *At the Defendant's Request.* At the arraignment or as soon afterward as practicable, the defendant may, in order to have an opportunity to move to suppress evidence under Rule 12(b)(3)(C), request notice of the government's intent to use (in its evidence-in-chief at trial) any evidence that the defendant may be entitled to discover under Rule 16.

**(c) Deadline for a Pretrial Motion; Consequences of Not Making a Timely Motion.**

**(1)** *Setting the Deadline.* The court may, at the arraignment or as soon afterward as practicable, set a deadline for the parties to make pretrial motions and may also schedule a motion hearing. If the court does not set one, the deadline is the start of trial.

**(2)** *Extending or Resetting the Deadline.* At any time before trial, the court may extend or reset the deadline for pretrial motions.

**(3)** *Consequences of Not Making a Timely Motion Under Rule 12(b)(3).* If a party does not meet the deadline for making a Rule 12(b)(3) motion, the motion is untimely. But a court may consider the defense, objection, or request if the party shows good cause.

**(d) Ruling on a Motion.** The court must decide every pretrial motion before trial unless it finds good cause to defer a ruling. The court must not defer ruling on a pretrial motion if the deferral will adversely affect a party's right to appeal. When factual issues are involved in deciding a motion, the court must state its essential findings on the record.

(e) [Reserved]

(f) **Recording the Proceedings.** All proceedings at a motion hearing, including any findings of fact and conclusions of law made orally by the court, must be recorded by a court reporter or a suitable recording device.

(g) **Defendant's Continued Custody or Release Status.** If the court grants a motion to dismiss based on a defect in instituting the prosecution, in the indictment, or in the information, it may order the defendant to be released or detained under 18 U.S.C. § 3142 for a specified time until a new indictment or information is filed. This rule does not affect any federal statutory period of limitations.

(h) **Producing Statements at a Suppression Hearing.** Rule 26.2 applies at a suppression hearing under Rule 12(b)(3)(C). At a suppression hearing, a law enforcement officer is considered a government witness.

## Rule 12.1.  Notice of an Alibi Defense

(a) **Government's Request for Notice and Defendant's Response.**

(1) *Government's Request.* An attorney for the government may request in writing that the

defendant notify an attorney for the government of any intended alibi defense. The request must state the time, date, and place of the alleged offense.

**(2)** *Defendant's Response.* Within 14 days after the request, or at some other time the court sets, the defendant must serve written notice on an attorney for the government of any intended alibi defense. The defendant's notice must state:

**(A)** each specific place where the defendant claims to have been at the time of the alleged offense; and

**(B)** the name, address, and telephone number of each alibi witness on whom the defendant intends to rely.

**(b) Disclosing Government Witnesses.**

**(1)** *Disclosure.*

**(A)** *In General.* If the defendant serves a Rule 12.1(a)(2) notice, an attorney for the government must disclose in writing to the defendant or the defendant's attorney:

**(i)** the name of each witness—and the address and telephone number of each witness other than a victim—that the government intends to rely on to establish that the defendant was present at the scene of the alleged offense; and

(ii) each government rebuttal witness to the defendant's alibi defense.

**(B)** *Victim's Address and Telephone Number.* If the government intends to rely on a victim's testimony to establish that the defendant was present at the scene of the alleged offense and the defendant establishes a need for the victim's address and telephone number, the court may:

(i) order the government to provide the information in writing to the defendant or the defendant's attorney; or

(ii) fashion a reasonable procedure that allows preparation of the defense and also protects the victim's interests.

**(2)** *Time to Disclose.* Unless the court directs otherwise, an attorney for the government must give its Rule 12.1(b)(1) disclosure within 14 days after the defendant serves notice of an intended alibi defense under Rule 12.1(a)(2), but no later than 14 days before trial.

**(c) Continuing Duty to Disclose.**

**(1)** *In General.* Both an attorney for the government and the defendant must promptly disclose in writing to the other party the name of each additional witness—and the address and telephone number of each additional witness other than a victim—if:

    **(A)** the disclosing party learns of the witness before or during trial; and

    **(B)** the witness should have been disclosed under Rule 12.1(a) or (b) if the disclosing party had known of the witness earlier.

  **(2)** *Address and Telephone Number of an Additional Victim Witness.* The address and telephone number of an additional victim witness must not be disclosed except as provided in Rule 12.1(b)(1)(B).

**(d) Exceptions.** For good cause, the court may grant an exception to any requirement of Rule 12.1(a)–(c).

**(e) Failure to Comply.** If a party fails to comply with this rule, the court may exclude the testimony of any undisclosed witness regarding the defendant's alibi. This rule does not limit the defendant's right to testify.

**(f) Inadmissibility of Withdrawn Intention.** Evidence of an intention to rely on an alibi defense, later withdrawn, or of a statement made in connection with that intention, is not, in any civil or criminal proceeding, admissible against the person who gave notice of the intention.

## Rule 12.2.  Notice of an Insanity Defense; Mental Examination

(a) **Notice of an Insanity Defense.** A defendant who intends to assert a defense of insanity at the time of the alleged offense must so notify an attorney for the government in writing within the time provided for filing a pretrial motion, or at any later time the court sets, and file a copy of the notice with the clerk. A defendant who fails to do so cannot rely on an insanity defense. The court may, for good cause, allow the defendant to file the notice late, grant additional trial-preparation time, or make other appropriate orders.

(b) **Notice of Expert Evidence of a Mental Condition.** If a defendant intends to introduce expert evidence relating to a mental disease or defect or any other mental condition of the defendant bearing on either (1) the issue of guilt or (2) the issue of punishment in a capital case, the defendant must—within the time provided for filing a pretrial motion or at any later time the court sets—notify an attorney for the government in writing of this intention and file a copy of the notice with the clerk. The court may, for good cause, allow the defendant to file the notice late, grant the parties additional trial-preparation time, or make other appropriate orders.

**(c) Mental Examination.**

(1) *Authority to Order an Examination; Procedures.*

**(A)** The court may order the defendant to submit to a competency examination under 18 U.S.C. § 4241.

**(B)** If the defendant provides notice under Rule 12.2(a), the court must, upon the government's motion, order the defendant to be examined under 18 U.S.C. § 4242. If the defendant provides notice under Rule 12.2(b) the court may, upon the government's motion, order the defendant to be examined under procedures ordered by the court.

(2) *Disclosing Results and Reports of Capital Sentencing Examination.* The results and reports of any examination conducted solely under Rule 12.2(c)(1) after notice under Rule 12.2(b)(2) must be sealed and must not be disclosed to any attorney for the government or the defendant unless the defendant is found guilty of one or more capital crimes and the defendant confirms an intent to offer during sentencing proceedings expert evidence on mental condition.

(3) *Disclosing Results and Reports of the Defendant's Expert Examination.* After disclosure under Rule 12.2(c)(2) of the results and reports

of the government's examination, the defendant must disclose to the government the results and reports of any examination on mental condition conducted by the defendant's expert about which the defendant intends to introduce expert evidence.

**(4)** *Inadmissibility of a Defendant's Statements.* No statement made by a defendant in the course of any examination conducted under this rule (whether conducted with or without the defendant's consent), no testimony by the expert based on the statement, and no other fruits of the statement may be admitted into evidence against the defendant in any criminal proceeding except on an issue regarding mental condition on which the defendant:

> **(A)** has introduced evidence of incompetency or evidence requiring notice under Rule 12.2(a) or (b)(1), or
>
> **(B)** has introduced expert evidence in a capital sentencing proceeding requiring notice under Rule 12.2(b)(2).

**(d) Failure to Comply.**

**(1)** *Failure to Give Notice or to Submit to Examination.* The court may exclude any expert evidence from the defendant on the issue of the defendant's mental disease, mental defect, or any other mental condition bearing on the defendant's guilt or the issue of punishment in a capital case if the defendant fails to:

**(A)** give notice under Rule 12.2(b); or

**(B)** submit to an examination when ordered under Rule 12.2(c).

**(2)** *Failure to Disclose.* The court may exclude any expert evidence for which the defendant has failed to comply with the disclosure requirement of Rule 12.2(c)(3).

**(e) Inadmissibility of Withdrawn Intention.** Evidence of an intention as to which notice was given under Rule 12.2(a) or (b), later withdrawn, is not, in any civil or criminal proceeding, admissible against the person who gave notice of the intention.

## Rule 12.3. Notice of a Public-Authority Defense

**(a) Notice of the Defense and Disclosure of Witnesses.**

**(1)** *Notice in General.* If a defendant intends to assert a defense of actual or believed exercise of public authority on behalf of a law enforcement agency or federal intelligence agency at the time of the alleged offense, the defendant must so notify an attorney for the government in writing and must file a copy of the notice with the clerk within the time provided for filing a pre-trial motion, or at any later time the court sets. The notice filed with the clerk must be under seal if the notice identifies a federal intelligence agency as the source of public authority.

(2) *Contents of Notice.* The notice must contain the following information:

(A) the law enforcement agency or federal intelligence agency involved;

(B) the agency member on whose behalf the defendant claims to have acted; and

(C) the time during which the defendant claims to have acted with public authority.

(3) *Response to the Notice.* An attorney for the government must serve a written response on the defendant or the defendant's attorney within 14 days after receiving the defendant's notice, but no later than 21 days before trial. The response must admit or deny that the defendant exercised the public authority identified in the defendant's notice.

(4) *Disclosing Witnesses.*

(A) *Government's Request.* An attorney for the government may request in writing that the defendant disclose the name, address, and telephone number of each witness the defendant intends to rely on to establish a public-authority defense. An attorney for the government may serve the request when the government serves its response to the defendant's notice under Rule 12.3(a)(3), or later, but must serve the request no later than 21 days before trial.

**(B)** *Defendant's Response.* Within 14 days after receiving the government's request, the defendant must serve on an attorney for the government a written statement of the name, address, and telephone number of each witness.

**(C)** *Government's Reply.* Within 14 days after receiving the defendant's statement, an attorney for the government must serve on the defendant or the defendant's attorney a written statement of the name of each witness—and the address and telephone number of each witness other than a victim—that the government intends to rely on to oppose the defendant's public-authority defense.

**(D)** *Victim's Address and Telephone Number.* If the government intends to rely on a victim's testimony to oppose the defendant's public-authority defense and the defendant establishes a need for the victim's address and telephone number, the court may:

(i) order the government to provide the information in writing to the defendant or the defendant's attorney; or

(ii) fashion a reasonable procedure that allows for preparing the defense and also protects the victim's interests.

(5) *Additional Time.* The court may, for good cause, allow a party additional time to comply with this rule.

(b) **Continuing Duty to Disclose.**

(1) *In General.* Both an attorney for the government and the defendant must promptly disclose in writing to the other party the name of any additional witness—and the address, and telephone number of any additional witness other than a victim—if:

(A) the disclosing party learns of the witness before or during trial; and

(B) the witness should have been disclosed under Rule 12.3(a)(4) if the disclosing party had known of the witness earlier.

(2) *Address and Telephone Number of an Additional Victim-Witness.* The address and telephone number of an additional victim-witness must not be disclosed except as provided in Rule 12.3(a)(4)(D).

(c) **Failure to Comply.** If a party fails to comply with this rule, the court may exclude the testimony of any undisclosed witness regarding the public-authority defense. This rule does not limit the defendant's right to testify.

(d) **Protective Procedures Unaffected.** This rule does not limit the court's authority to issue appropriate protective orders or to order that any filings be under seal.

(e) **Inadmissibility of Withdrawn Intention.** Evidence of an intention as to which notice was given under Rule 12.3(a), later withdrawn, is not, in any civil or criminal proceeding, admissible against the person who gave notice of the intention.

## Rule 12.4. Disclosure Statement

(a) **Who Must File.**

(1) *Nongovernmental Corporate Party.* Any nongovernmental corporate party to a proceeding in a district court must file a statement that identifies any parent corporation and any publicly held corporation that owns 10% or more of its stock or states that there is no such corporation.

(2) *Organizational Victim.* Unless the government shows good cause, it must file a statement identifying any organizational victim of the alleged criminal activity. If the organizational

victim is a corporation, the statement must also
disclose the information required by Rule 12.4(a)
(1) to the extent it can be obtained through due
diligence.

(b)  **Time for Filing; Supplemental Filing.** A party
must:

(1) file the Rule 12.4(a) statement within 28
days after the defendant's initial appearance; and

(2) promptly file a later statement if any required information changes.

## Rule 13.   Joint Trial of Separate Cases

The court may order that separate cases be tried
together as though brought in a single indictment or
information if all offenses and all defendants could
have been joined in a single indictment or information.

## Rule 14.   Relief from Prejudicial
##            Joinder

(a)  **Relief.** If the joinder of offenses or defendants
in an indictment, an information, or a consolida-
tion for trial appears to prejudice a defendant or the
government, the court may order separate trials of
counts, sever the defendants' trials, or provide any
other relief that justice requires.

(b)  **Defendant's Statements.** Before ruling on a
defendant's motion to sever, the court may order an
attorney for the government to deliver to the court

for in camera inspection any defendant's statement that the government intends to use as evidence.

## Rule 15.  Depositions

(a) **When Taken.**

(1) *In General.* A party may move that a prospective witness be deposed in order to preserve testimony for trial. The court may grant the motion because of exceptional circumstances and in the interest of justice. If the court orders the deposition to be taken, it may also require the deponent to produce at the deposition any designated material that is not privileged, including any book, paper, document, record, recording, or data.

(2) *Detained Material Witness.* A witness who is detained under 18 U.S.C. § 3144 may request to be deposed by filing a written motion and giving notice to the parties. The court may then order that the deposition be taken and may discharge the witness after the witness has signed under oath the deposition transcript.

(b) **Notice.**

(1) *In General.* A party seeking to take a deposition must give every other party reasonable written notice of the deposition's date and location. The notice must state the name and address of

each deponent. If requested by a party receiving the notice, the court may, for good cause, change the deposition's date or location.

**(2)** *To the Custodial Officer.* A party seeking to take the deposition must also notify the officer who has custody of the defendant of the scheduled date and location.

**(c) Defendant's Presence.**

**(1)** *Defendant in Custody.* Except as authorized by Rule 15(c)(3), the officer who has custody of the defendant must produce the defendant at the deposition and keep the defendant in the witness's presence during the examination, unless the defendant:

**(A)** waives in writing the right to be present; or

**(B)** persists in disruptive conduct justifying exclusion after being warned by the court that disruptive conduct will result in the defendant's exclusion.

**(2)** *Defendant Not in Custody.* Except as authorized by Rule 15(c)(3), a defendant who is not in custody has the right upon request to be present at the deposition, subject to any conditions imposed by the court. If the government tenders the defendant's expenses as provided in Rule

15(d) but the defendant still fails to appear, the defendant—absent good cause—waives both the right to appear and any objection to the taking and use of the deposition based on that right.

(3) *Taking Depositions Outside the United States Without the Defendant's Presence.* The deposition of a witness who is outside the United States may be taken without the defendant's presence if the court makes case-specific findings of all the following:

(A) the witness's testimony could provide substantial proof of a material fact in a felony prosecution;

(B) there is a substantial likelihood that the witness's attendance at trial cannot be obtained;

(C) the witness's presence for a deposition in the United States cannot be obtained;

(D) the defendant cannot be present because:

(i) the country where the witness is located will not permit the defendant to attend the deposition;

(ii) for an in-custody defendant, secure transportation and continuing custody cannot be assured at the witness's location; or

(iii) for an out-of-custody defendant, no reasonable conditions will assure an appearance at the deposition or at trial or sentencing; and

(E) the defendant can meaningfully participate in the deposition through reasonable means.

(d) **Expenses.** If the deposition was requested by the government, the court may—or if the defendant is unable to bear the deposition expenses, the court must—order the government to pay:

(1) any reasonable travel and subsistence expenses of the defendant and the defendant's attorney to attend the deposition; and

(2) the costs of the deposition transcript.

(e) **Manner of Taking.** Unless these rules or a court order provides otherwise, a deposition must be taken and filed in the same manner as a deposition in a civil action, except that:

(1) A defendant may not be deposed without that defendant's consent.

(2) The scope and manner of the deposition examination and cross-examination must be the same as would be allowed during trial.

(3) The government must provide to the defendant or the defendant's attorney, for use at

the deposition, any statement of the deponent in the government's possession to which the defendant would be entitled at trial.

**(f) Admissibility and Use as Evidence.** An order authorizing a deposition to be taken under this rule does not determine its admissibility. A party may use all or part of a deposition as provided by the Federal Rules of Evidence.

**(g) Objections.** A party objecting to deposition testimony or evidence must state the grounds for the objection during the deposition.

## Rule 16. Discovery and Inspection

(a) **Government's Disclosure.**

(1) *Information Subject to Disclosure.*

(A) *Defendant's Oral Statement.* Upon a defendant's request, the government must disclose to the defendant the substance of any relevant oral statement made by the defendant, before or after arrest, in response to interrogation by a person the defendant knew was a government agent if the government intends to use the statement at trial.

(B) *Defendant's Written or Recorded Statement.* Upon a defendant's request, the government must disclose to the defendant, and make available for inspection, copying, or photo-graphing, all of the following:

(i) any relevant written or recorded state-ment by the defendant if:

- the statement is within the govern-ment's possession, custody, or control; and

- the attorney for the government knows—or through due diligence could know—that the statement exists;

(ii) the portion of any written record con-taining the substance of any relevant oral statement made before or after arrest if the defendant made the statement in response to interrogation by a person the defendant knew was a government agent; and

(iii) the defendant's recorded testimony before a grand jury relating to the charged offense.

(C) *Organizational Defendant.* Upon a defen-dant's request, if the defendant is an organi-zation, the government must disclose to the defendant any statement described in Rule 16(a)(1)(A) and (B) if the government con-tends that the person making the statement:

(i) was legally able to bind the defendant regarding the subject of the statement because of that person's position as the defendant's director, officer, employee, or agent; or

(ii) was personally involved in the alleged conduct constituting the offense and was legally able to bind the defendant regarding that conduct because of that person's position as the defendant's director, officer, employee, or agent.

**(D)** *Defendant's Prior Record.* Upon a defendant's request, the government must furnish the defendant with a copy of the defendant's prior criminal record that is within the government's possession, custody, or control if the attorney for the government knows—or through due diligence could know—that the record exists.

**(E)** *Documents and Objects.* Upon a defendant's request, the government must permit the defendant to inspect and to copy or photograph books, papers, documents, data, photographs, tangible objects, buildings or places, or copies or portions of any of these items, if the item is within the government's possession, custody, or control and:

(i) the item is material to preparing the defense;

(ii) the government intends to use the item in its case-in-chief at trial; or

(iii) the item was obtained from or belongs to the defendant.

**(F)** *Reports of Examinations and Tests.* Upon a defendant's request, the government must permit a defendant to inspect and to copy or photograph the results or reports of any physical or mental examination and of any scientific test or experiment if:

(i) the item is within the government's possession, custody, or control;

(ii) the attorney for the government knows—or through due diligence could know—that the item exists; and

(iii) the item is material to preparing the defense or the government intends to use the item in its case-in-chief at trial.

**(G)** *Expert Witnesses.* At the defendant's request, the government must give to the defendant a written summary of any testimony that the government intends to use under Rules 702, 703, or 705 of the Federal Rules of Evidence during its case-in-chief at trial. If the government requests discovery under subdivision (b)(1)(C)(ii) and the defendant complies, the government must, at the defendant's request, give to the defendant a written summary of testimony that the government intends to use under Rules 702, 703, or 705 of the Federal Rules of Evidence as evidence at trial on the issue of the defendant's mental condition. The summary provided under this subparagraph must describe the witness's opinions, the bases and reasons for those opinions, and the witness's qualifications.

(2) *Information Not Subject to Disclosure.* Except as permitted by Rule 16(a)(1) (A)–(D), (F), and (G), this rule does not authorize the discovery or inspection of reports, memoranda, or other internal government documents made by an attorney for the government or other government agent in connection with investigating or prosecuting the case. Nor does this rule authorize the discovery or inspection of statements made by prospective government witnesses except as provided in 18 U.S.C. § 3500.

(3) *Grand Jury Transcripts.* This rule does not apply to the discovery or inspection of a grand jury's recorded proceedings, except as provided in Rules 6, 12(h), 16(a)(1), and 26.2.

(b) **Defendant's Disclosure.**

(1) *Information Subject to Disclosure.*

(A) *Documents and Objects.* If a defendant requests disclosure under Rule 16(a)(1)(E) and the government complies, then the defendant must permit the government, upon request, to inspect and to copy or photograph books, papers, documents, data, photographs, tangible objects, buildings or places, or copies or portions of any of these items if:

(i) the item is within the defendant's possession, custody, or control; and

(ii) the defendant intends to use the item in the defendant's case-in-chief at trial.

(B) *Reports of Examinations and Tests.* If a defendant requests disclosure under Rule 16(a)(1)(F) and the government complies, the defendant must permit the government, upon request, to inspect and to copy or photograph the results or reports of any physical or mental examination and of any scientific test or experiment if:

(i) the item is within the defendant's possession, custody, or control; and

(ii) the defendant intends to use the item in the defendant's case-in-chief at trial, or intends to call the witness who prepared the report and the report relates to the witness's testimony.

(C) *Expert Witnesses.* The defendant must, at the government's request, give to the government a written summary of any testimony that the defendant intends to use under Rules 702, 703, or 705 of the Federal Rules of Evidence as evidence at trial, if—

(i) the defendant requests disclosure under subdivision (a)(1)(G) and the government complies; or

(ii) the defendant has given notice under Rule 12.2(b) of an intent to present expert testimony on the defendant's mental condition.

This summary must describe the witness's opinions, the bases and reasons for those opinions, and the witness's qualifications.

(2) *Information Not Subject to Disclosure.* Except for scientific or medical reports, Rule 16(b)(1) does not authorize discovery or inspection of:

(A) reports, memoranda, or other documents made by the defendant, or the defendant's attorney or agent, during the case's investigation or defense; or

**(B)** a statement made to the defendant, or the defendant's attorney or agent, by:

　**(i)** the defendant;

　**(ii)** a government or defense witness; or

　**(iii)** a prospective government or defense witness.

**(c) Continuing Duty to Disclose.** A party who discovers additional evidence or material before or during trial must promptly disclose its existence to the other party or the court if:

　**(1)** the evidence or material is subject to discovery or inspection under this rule; and

　**(2)** the other party previously requested, or the court ordered, its production.

**(d) Regulating Discovery.**

　**(1)** *Protective and Modifying Orders.* At any time the court may, for good cause, deny, restrict, or defer discovery or inspection, or grant other appropriate relief. The court may permit a party to show good cause by a written statement that the court will inspect ex parte. If relief is granted, the court must preserve the entire text of the party's statement under seal.

**(2)** *Failure to Comply.* If a party fails to comply with this rule, the court may:

 **(A)** order that party to permit the discovery or inspection; specify its time, place, and manner; and prescribe other just terms and conditions;

 **(B)** grant a continuance;

 **(C)** prohibit that party from introducing the undisclosed evidence; or

 **(D)** enter any other order that is just under the circumstances.

## Rule 16.1. Pretrial Discovery Conference; Request for Court Action

**(a) Discovery Conference.** No later than 14 days after the arraignment, the attorney for the government and the defendant's attorney must confer and try to agree on a timetable and procedures for pretrial disclosure under Rule 16.

**(b) Request for Court Action.** After the discovery conference, one or both parties may ask the court to determine or modify the time, place, manner, or other aspects of disclosure to facilitate preparation for trial.

## Rule 17. Subpoena

**(a) Content.** A subpoena must state the court's name and the title of the proceeding, include the seal of the court, and command the witness to attend and testify at the time and place the subpoena specifies. The clerk must issue a blank subpoena—signed and sealed—to the party requesting it, and that party must fill in the blanks before the subpoena is served.

**(b) Defendant Unable to Pay.** Upon a defendant's ex parte application, the court must order that a subpoena be issued for a named witness if the defendant shows an inability to pay the witness's fees and the necessity of the witness's presence for an adequate defense. If the court orders a subpoena to be issued, the process costs and witness fees will be paid in the same manner as those paid for witnesses the government subpoenas.

**(c) Producing Documents and Objects.**

(1) *In General.* A subpoena may order the witness to produce any books, papers, documents, data, or other objects the subpoena designates. The court may direct the witness to produce the designated items in court before trial or before they are to be offered in evidence. When the items arrive, the court may permit the parties and their attorneys to inspect all or part of them.

(2) *Quashing or Modifying the Subpoena.* On motion made promptly, the court may quash or modify the subpoena if compliance would be unreasonable or oppressive.

(3) *Subpoena for Personal or Confidential Information About a Victim.* After a complaint,

indictment, or information is filed, a subpoena
requiring the production of personal or confidential information about a victim may be served on
a third party only by court order. Before entering
the order and unless there are exceptional circumstances, the court must require giving notice to
the victim so that the victim can move to quash
or modify the subpoena or otherwise object.

(d) **Service.** A marshal, a deputy marshal, or any nonparty who is at least 18 years old may serve a subpoena.
The server must deliver a copy of the subpoena to the
witness and must tender to the witness one day's wit-
ness-attendance fee and the legal mileage allowance.
The server need not tender the attendance fee or mileage allowance when the United States, a federal officer,
or a federal agency has requested the subpoena.

(e) **Place of Service.**

(1) *In the United States.* A subpoena requiring a
witness to attend a hearing or trial may be served
at any place within the United States.

(2) *In a Foreign Country.* If the witness is in a
foreign country, 28 U.S.C. § 1783 governs the
subpoena's service.

(f) **Issuing a Deposition Subpoena.**

(1) *Issuance.* A court order to take a deposition
authorizes the clerk in the district where the

deposition is to be taken to issue a subpoena for any witness named or described in the order.

(2) *Place.* After considering the convenience of the witness and the parties, the court may order—and the subpoena may require—the witness to appear anywhere the court designates.

(g) **Contempt.** The court (other than a magistrate judge) may hold in contempt a witness who, without adequate excuse, disobeys a subpoena issued by a federal court in that district. A magistrate judge may hold in contempt a witness who, without adequate excuse, disobeys a subpoena issued by that magistrate judge as provided in 28 U.S.C. § 636(e).

(h) **Information Not Subject to a Subpoena.** No party may subpoena a statement of a witness or of a prospective witness under this rule. Rule 26.2 governs the production of the statement.

## Rule 17.1.   Pretrial Conference

On its own, or on a party's motion, the court may hold one or more pretrial conferences to promote a fair and expeditious trial. When a conference ends, the court must prepare and file a memorandum of any matters agreed to during the conference. The government may not use any statement made during the conference by the defendant or the defendant's attorney unless it is in writing and is signed by the defendant and the defendant's attorney.

# TITLE V.  VENUE

## Rule 18.  Place of Prosecution and Trial

Unless a statute or these rules permit otherwise, the government must prosecute an offense in a district where the offense was committed. The court must set the place of trial within the district with due regard for the convenience of the defendant, any victim, and the witnesses, and the prompt administration of justice.

## Rule 19.  [Reserved]

## Rule 20.  Transfer for Plea and Sentence

(a) **Consent to Transfer.** A prosecution may be transferred from the district where the indictment or information is pending, or from which a warrant on a complaint has been issued, to the district where the defendant is arrested, held, or present if:

(1) the defendant states in writing a wish to plead guilty or nolo contendere and to waive trial in the district where the indictment, information, or complaint is pending, consents in writing to the court's disposing of the case in the transferee district, and files the statement in the transferee district; and

(2) the United States attorneys in both districts approve the transfer in writing.

(b) **Clerk's Duties.** After receiving the defendant's statement and the required approvals, the clerk where the indictment, information, or complaint is pending must send the file, or a certified copy, to the clerk in the transferee district.

(c) **Effect of a Not Guilty Plea.** If the defendant pleads not guilty after the case has been transferred under Rule 20(a), the clerk must return the papers to the court where the prosecution began, and that court must restore the proceeding to its docket. The defendant's statement that the defendant wished to plead guilty or nolo contendere is not, in any civil or criminal proceeding, admissible against the defendant.

(d) **Juveniles.**

(1) *Consent to Transfer.* A juvenile, as defined in 18 U.S.C. § 5031, may be proceeded against as a juvenile delinquent in the district where the juvenile is arrested, held, or present if:

(A) the alleged offense that occurred in the other district is not punishable by death or life imprisonment;

(B) an attorney has advised the juvenile;

(C) the court has informed the juvenile of the juvenile's rights—including the right to be returned to the district where the offense allegedly occurred—and the consequences of waiving those rights;

(D) the juvenile, after receiving the court's information about rights, consents in writing to be proceeded against in the transferee district, and files the consent in the transferee district;

(E) the United States attorneys for both districts approve the transfer in writing; and

(F) the transferee court approves the transfer.

(2) *Clerk's Duties.* After receiving the juvenile's written consent and the required approvals, the clerk where the indictment, information, or complaint is pending or where the alleged offense occurred must send the file, or a certified copy, to the clerk in the transferee district.

## Rule 21.   Transfer for Trial

(a) **For Prejudice.** Upon the defendant's motion, the court must transfer the proceeding against that defendant to another district if the court is satisfied that so great a prejudice against the defendant exists in the transferring district that the defendant cannot obtain a fair and impartial trial there.

**(b) For Convenience.** Upon the defendant's motion, the court may transfer the proceeding, or one or more counts, against that defendant to another district for the convenience of the parties, any victim, and the witnesses, and in the interest of justice.

**(c) Proceedings on Transfer.** When the court orders a transfer, the clerk must send to the transferee district the file, or a certified copy, and any bail taken. The prosecution will then continue in the transferee district.

**(d) Time to File a Motion to Transfer.** A motion to transfer may be made at or before arraignment or at any other time the court or these rules prescribe.

# TITLE VI.    TRIAL

## Rule 23.    Jury or Nonjury Trial

(a) **Jury Trial.** If the defendant is entitled to a jury trial, the trial must be by jury unless:

(1) the defendant waives a jury trial in writing;

(2) the government consents; and

(3) the court approves.

(b) **Jury Size.**

(1) *In General.* A jury consists of 12 persons unless this rule provides otherwise.

(2) *Stipulation for a Smaller Jury.* At any time before the verdict, the parties may, with the court's approval, stipulate in writing that:

(A) the jury may consist of fewer than 12 persons; or

(B) a jury of fewer than 12 persons may return a verdict if the court finds it necessary to excuse a juror for good cause after the trial begins.

(3) *Court Order for a Jury of 11.* After the jury has retired to deliberate, the court may permit a jury of 11 persons to return a verdict, even without a stipulation by the parties, if the court finds good cause to excuse a juror.

(c) **Nonjury Trial.** In a case tried without a jury, the court must find the defendant guilty or not guilty. If a party requests before the finding of guilty or not guilty, the court must state its specific findings of fact in open court or in a written decision or opinion.

## Rule 24. Trial Jurors

(a) **Examination.**

 (1) *In General.* The court may examine prospective jurors or may permit the attorneys for the parties to do so.

 (2) *Court Examination.* If the court examines the jurors, it must permit the attorneys for the parties to:

  (A) ask further questions that the court considers proper; or

  (B) submit further questions that the court may ask if it considers them proper.

(b) **Peremptory Challenges.** Each side is entitled to the number of peremptory challenges to prospective jurors specified below. The court may allow additional peremptory challenges to multiple defendants, and may allow the defendants to exercise those challenges separately or jointly.

(1) *Capital Case.* Each side has 20 peremptory challenges when the government seeks the death penalty.

(2) *Other Felony Case.* The government has 6 peremptory challenges and the defendant or defendants jointly have 10 peremptory challenges when the defendant is charged with a crime punishable by imprisonment of more than one year.

(3) *Misdemeanor Case.* Each side has 3 peremptory challenges when the defendant is charged with a crime punishable by fine, imprisonment of one year or less, or both.

(c) **Alternate Jurors.**

(1) *In General.* The court may impanel up to 6 alternate jurors to replace any jurors who are unable to perform or who are disqualified from performing their duties.

(2) *Procedure.*

(A) Alternate jurors must have the same qualifications and be selected and sworn in the same manner as any other juror.

(B) Alternate jurors replace jurors in the same sequence in which the alternates were selected. An alternate juror who replaces a juror has the same authority as the other jurors.

(3) *Retaining Alternate Jurors.* The court may retain alternate jurors after the jury retires to deliberate. The court must ensure that a retained alternate does not discuss the case with anyone until that alternate replaces a juror or is discharged. If an alternate replaces a juror after deliberations have begun, the court must instruct the jury to begin its deliberations anew.

(4) *Peremptory Challenges.* Each side is entitled to the number of additional peremptory challenges to prospective alternate jurors specified below. These additional challenges may be used only to remove alternate jurors.

(A) *One or Two Alternates.* One additional peremptory challenge is permitted when one or two alternates are impaneled.

(B) *Three or Four Alternates.* Two additional peremptory challenges are permitted when three or four alternates are impaneled.

(C) *Five or Six Alternates.* Three additional peremptory challenges are permitted when five or six alternates are impaneled.

## Rule 25.  Judge's Disability

(a) **During Trial.** Any judge regularly sitting in or assigned to the court may complete a jury trial if:

(1) the judge before whom the trial began cannot proceed because of death, sickness, or other disability; and

(2) the judge completing the trial certifies familiarity with the trial record.

(b) **After a Verdict or Finding of Guilty.**

(1) *In General.* After a verdict or finding of guilty, any judge regularly sitting in or assigned to a court may complete the court's duties if the judge who presided at trial cannot perform those duties because of absence, death, sickness, or other disability.

(2) *Granting a New Trial.* The successor judge may grant a new trial if satisfied that:

(A) a judge other than the one who presided at the trial cannot perform the post-trial duties; or

(B) a new trial is necessary for some other reason.

## Rule 26. Taking Testimony

In every trial the testimony of witnesses must be taken in open court, unless otherwise provided by a statute or by rules adopted under 28 U.S.C. §§ 2072–2077.

## Rule 26.1.   Foreign Law Determination

A party intending to raise an issue of foreign law must provide the court and all parties with reasonable written notice. Issues of foreign law are questions of law, but in deciding such issues a court may consider any relevant material or source—including testimony—without regard to the Federal Rules of Evidence.

## Rule 26.2.   Producing a Witness's Statement

(a) **Motion to Produce.** After a witness other than the defendant has testified on direct examination, the court, on motion of a party who did not call the witness, must order an attorney for the government or the defendant and the defendant's attorney to produce, for the examination and use of the moving party, any statement of the witness that is in their possession and that relates to the subject matter of the witness's testimony.

(b) **Producing the Entire Statement.** If the entire statement relates to the subject matter of the witness's testimony, the court must order that the statement be delivered to the moving party.

(c) **Producing a Redacted Statement.** If the party who called the witness claims that the statement contains information that is privileged or does not relate to the subject matter of the witness's testimony, the court must inspect the statement in camera.

After excising any privileged or unrelated portions, the court must order delivery of the redacted statement to the moving party. If the defendant objects to an excision, the court must preserve the entire statement with the excised portion indicated, under seal, as part of the record.

**(d) Recess to Examine a Statement.** The court may recess the proceedings to allow time for a party to examine the statement and prepare for its use.

**(e) Sanction for Failure to Produce or Deliver a Statement.** If the party who called the witness disobeys an order to produce or deliver a statement, the court must strike the witness's testimony from the record. If an attorney for the government disobeys the order, the court must declare a mistrial if justice so requires.

**(f) "Statement" Defined.** As used in this rule, a witness's "statement" means:

(1) a written statement that the witness makes and signs, or otherwise adopts or approves;

(2) a substantially verbatim, contemporaneously recorded recital of the witness's oral statement that is contained in any recording or any transcription of a recording; or

(3) the witness's statement to a grand jury, however taken or recorded, or a transcription of such a statement.

(g) **Scope.** This rule applies at trial, at a suppression hearing under Rule 12, and to the extent specified in the following rules:

(1) Rule 5.1(h) (preliminary hearing);

(2) Rule 32(i)(2) (sentencing);

(3) Rule 32.1(e) (hearing to revoke or modify probation for supervised release);

(4) Rule 46(j) (detention hearing); and

(5) Rule 8 of the Rules Governing Proceedings under 28 U.S.C. § 2255.

## Rule 26.3.   Mistrial

Before ordering a mistrial, the court must give each defendant and the government an opportunity to comment on the propriety of the order, to state whether that party consents or objects, and to suggest alternatives.

## Rule 27.   Proving an Official Record

A party may prove an official record, an entry in such a record, or the lack of a record or entry in the same manner as in a civil action.

## Rule 28.   Interpreters

The court may select, appoint, and set the reasonable compensation for an interpreter. The compensation must be paid from funds provided by law or by the government, as the court may direct.

## Rule 29. Motion for a Judgment of Acquittal

(a) **Before Submission to the Jury.** After the government closes its evidence or after the close of all the evidence, the court on the defendant's motion must enter a judgment of acquittal of any offense for which the evidence is insufficient to sustain a conviction. The court may on its own consider whether the evidence is insufficient to sustain a conviction. If the court denies a motion for a judgment of acquittal at the close of the government's evidence, the defendant may offer evidence without having reserved the right to do so.

(b) **Reserving Decision.** The court may reserve decision on the motion, proceed with the trial (where the motion is made before the close of all the evidence), submit the case to the jury, and decide the motion either before the jury returns a verdict or after it returns a verdict of guilty or is discharged without having returned a verdict. If the court reserves decision, it must decide the motion on the basis of the evidence at the time the ruling was reserved.

(c) **After Jury Verdict or Discharge.**

(1) *Time for a Motion.* A defendant may move for a judgment of acquittal, or renew such a mo-

tion, within 14 days after a guilty verdict or after the court discharges the jury, whichever is later.

**(2)** *Ruling on the Motion.* If the jury has returned a guilty verdict, the court may set aside the verdict and enter an acquittal. If the jury has failed to return a verdict, the court may enter a judgment of acquittal.

**(3)** *No Prior Motion Required.* A defendant is not required to move for a judgment of acquittal before the court submits the case to the jury as a prerequisite for making such a motion after jury discharge.

**(d) Conditional Ruling on a Motion for a New Trial.**

**(1)** *Motion for a New Trial.* If the court enters a judgment of acquittal after a guilty verdict, the court must also conditionally determine whether any motion for a new trial should be granted if the judgment of acquittal is later vacated or reversed. The court must specify the reasons for that determination.

**(2)** *Finality.* The court's order conditionally granting a motion for a new trial does not affect the finality of the judgment of acquittal.

**(3)** *Appeal.*

**(A)** *Grant of a Motion for a New Trial.* If the court conditionally grants a motion for a new trial and an appellate court later reverses the judgment of acquittal, the trial court must proceed with the new trial unless the appellate court orders otherwise.

**(B)** *Denial of a Motion for a New Trial.* If the court conditionally denies a motion for a new trial, an appellee may assert that the denial was erroneous. If the appellate court later reverses the judgment of acquittal, the trial court must proceed as the appellate court directs.

## Rule 29.1.   Closing Argument

Closing arguments proceed in the following order:

(a) the government argues;

(b) the defense argues; and

(c) the government rebuts.

## Rule 30.   Jury Instructions

(a) **In General.** Any party may request in writing that the court instruct the jury on the law as specified in the request. The request must be made at the close of the evidence or at any earlier time that the court reasonably sets. When the request is made, the requesting party must furnish a copy to every other party.

**(b) Ruling on a Request.** The court must inform the parties before closing arguments how it intends to rule on the requested instructions.

**(c) Time for Giving Instructions.** The court may instruct the jury before or after the arguments are completed, or at both times.

**(d) Objections to Instructions.** A party who objects to any portion of the instructions or to a failure to give a requested instruction must inform the court of the specific objection and the grounds for the objection before the jury retires to deliberate. An opportunity must be given to object out of the jury's hearing and, on request, out of the jury's presence. Failure to object in accordance with this rule precludes appellate review, except as permitted under Rule 52(b).

## Rule 31.  Jury Verdict

**(a) Return.** The jury must return its verdict to a judge in open court. The verdict must be unanimous.

**(b) Partial Verdicts, Mistrial, and Retrial.**

(1) *Multiple Defendants.* If there are multiple defendants, the jury may return a verdict at any time during its deliberations as to any defendant about whom it has agreed.

(2) *Multiple Counts.* If the jury cannot agree on all counts as to any defendant, the jury may return a verdict on those counts on which it has agreed.

(3) *Mistrial and Retrial.* If the jury cannot agree on a verdict on one or more counts, the court may declare a mistrial on those counts. The government may retry any defendant on any count on which the jury could not agree.

(c) **Lesser Offense or Attempt.** A defendant may be found guilty of any of the following:

(1) an offense necessarily included in the offense charged;

(2) an attempt to commit the offense charged; or

(3) an attempt to commit an offense necessarily included in the offense charged, if the attempt is an offense in its own right.

(d) **Jury Poll.** After a verdict is returned but before the jury is discharged, the court must on a party's request, or may on its own, poll the jurors individually. If the poll reveals a lack of unanimity, the court may direct the jury to deliberate further or may declare a mistrial and discharge the jury.

# TITLE VII.   POST-CONVICTION PROCEDURES

## Rule 32.   Sentencing and Judgment

(a) [Reserved.]

(b) Time of Sentencing.

(1) *In General.* The court must impose sentence without unnecessary delay.

(2) *Changing Time Limits.* The court may, for good cause, change any time limits prescribed in this rule.

(c) Presentence Investigation.

(1) *Required Investigation.*

(A) *In General.* The probation officer must conduct a presentence investigation and submit a report to the court before it imposes sentence unless:

(i)  18 U.S.C. § 3593(c) or another statute requires otherwise; or

(ii)  the court finds that the information in the record enables it to meaningfully exercise its sentencing authority under 18 U.S.C. § 3553, and the court explains its finding on the record.

(B) *Restitution.* If the law permits restitution, the probation officer must conduct an investigation and submit a report that contains sufficient information for the court to order restitution.

**(2)** *Interviewing the Defendant.* The probation officer who interviews a defendant as part of a presentence investigation must, on request, give the defendant's attorney notice and a reasonable opportunity to attend the interview.

**(d) Presentence Report.**

**(1)** *Applying the Advisory Sentencing Guidelines.* The presentence report must:

**(A)** identify all applicable guidelines and policy statements of the Sentencing Commission;

**(B)** calculate the defendant's offense level and criminal history category;

**(C)** state the resulting sentencing range and kinds of sentences available;

**(D)** identify any factor relevant to:

(i) the appropriate kind of sentence, or

(ii) the appropriate sentence within the applicable sentencing range; and

**(E)** identify any basis for departing from the applicable sentencing range.

**(2)** *Additional Information.* The presentence report must also contain the following:

(A) the defendant's history and characteristics, including:

(i) any prior criminal record;

(ii) the defendant's financial condition; and

(iii) any circumstances affecting the defendant's behavior that may be helpful in imposing sentence or in correctional treatment;

(B) information that assesses any financial, social, psychological, and medical impact on any victim;

(C) when appropriate, the nature and extent of nonprison programs and resources available to the defendant;

(D) when the law provides for restitution, information sufficient for a restitution order;

(E) if the court orders a study under 18 U.S.C. § 3552(b), any resulting report and recommendation;

(F) a statement of whether the government seeks forfeiture under Rule 32.2 and any other law; and

(G) any other information that the court requires, including information relevant to the factors under 18 U.S.C. § 3553(a).

**(3)** *Exclusions.* The presentence report must exclude the following:

**(A)** any diagnoses that, if disclosed, might seriously disrupt a rehabilitation program;

**(B)** any sources of information obtained upon a promise of confidentiality; and

**(C)** any other information that, if disclosed, might result in physical or other harm to the defendant or others.

**(e) Disclosing the Report and Recommendation.**

**(1)** *Time to Disclose.* Unless the defendant has consented in writing, the probation officer must not submit a presentence report to the court or disclose its contents to anyone until the defendant has pleaded guilty or nolo contendere, or has been found guilty.

**(2)** *Minimum Required Notice.* The probation officer must give the presentence report to the defendant, the defendant's attorney, and an attorney for the government at least 35 days before sentencing unless the defendant waives this minimum period.

**(3)** *Sentence Recommendation.* By local rule or by order in a case, the court may direct the probation officer not to disclose to anyone other than the court the officer's recommendation on the sentence.

**(f) Objecting to the Report.**

(1) *Time to Object.* Within 14 days after receiving the presentence report, the parties must state in writing any objections, including objections to material information, sentencing guideline ranges, and policy statements contained in or omitted from the report.

(2) *Serving Objections.* An objecting party must provide a copy of its objections to the opposing party and to the probation officer.

(3) *Action on Objections.* After receiving objections, the probation officer may meet with the parties to discuss the objections. The probation officer may then investigate further and revise the presentence report as appropriate.

**(g) Submitting the Report.** At least 7 days before sentencing, the probation officer must submit to the court and to the parties the presentence report and an addendum containing any unresolved objections, the grounds for those objections, and the probation officer's comments on them.

**(h) Notice of Possible Departure from Sentencing Guidelines.** Before the court may depart from the applicable sentencing range on a ground not identified for departure either in the presentence report or in a party's prehearing submission, the court must give the parties reasonable notice that it is contemplating such a departure. The notice must specify any ground on which the court is contemplating a departure.

**(i) Sentencing.**

   **(1)** *In General.* At sentencing, the court:

   **(A)** must verify that the defendant and the defendant's attorney have read and discussed the presentence report and any addendum to the report;

   **(B)** must give to the defendant and an attorney for the government a written summary of—or summarize in camera—any information excluded from the presentence report under Rule 32(d)(3) on which the court will rely in sentencing, and give them a reasonable opportunity to comment on that information;

   **(C)** must allow the parties' attorneys to comment on the probation officer's determinations and other matters relating to an appropriate sentence; and

   **(D)** may, for good cause, allow a party to make a new objection at any time before sentence is imposed.

(2) *Introducing Evidence; Producing a Statement.* The court may permit the parties to introduce evidence on the objections. If a witness testifies at sentencing, Rule 26.2(a)–(d) and (f) applies. If a party fails to comply with a Rule 26.2 order to produce a witness's statement, the court must not consider that witness's testimony.

(3) *Court Determinations.* At sentencing, the court:

(A)  may accept any undisputed portion of the presentence report as a finding of fact;

(B)  must—for any disputed portion of the presentence report or other controverted matter—rule on the dispute or determine that a ruling is unnecessary either because the matter will not affect sentencing, or because the court will not consider the matter in sentencing; and

(C)  must append a copy of the court's determinations under this rule to any copy of the presentence report made available to the Bureau of Prisons.

(4) *Opportunity to Speak.*

(A) *By a Party.* Before imposing sentence, the court must:

(i) provide the defendant's attorney an opportunity to speak on the defendant's behalf;

(ii) address the defendant personally in order to permit the defendant to speak or present any information to mitigate the sentence; and

(iii) provide an attorney for the government an opportunity to speak equivalent to that of the defendant's attorney.

**(B)** *By a Victim.* Before imposing sentence, the court must address any victim of the crime who is present at sentencing and must permit the victim to be reasonably heard.

**(C)** *In Camera Proceedings.* Upon a party's motion and for good cause, the court may hear in camera any statement made under Rule 32(i)(4).

**(j) Defendant's Right to Appeal.**

(1) *Advice of a Right to Appeal.*

**(A)** *Appealing a Conviction.* If the defendant pleaded not guilty and was convicted, after sentencing the court must advise the defendant of the right to appeal the conviction.

**(B)** *Appealing a Sentence.* After sentencing— regardless of the defendant's plea—the court must advise the defendant of any right to appeal the sentence.

(**C**) *Appeal Costs.* The court must advise a defendant who is unable to pay appeal costs of the right to ask for permission to appeal in forma pauperis.

(2) *Clerk's Filing of Notice.* If the defendant so requests, the clerk must immediately prepare and file a notice of appeal on the defendant's behalf.

(**k**) **Judgment.**

(1) *In General.* In the judgment of conviction, the court must set forth the plea, the jury verdict or the court's findings, the adjudication, and the sentence. If the defendant is found not guilty or is otherwise entitled to be discharged, the court must so order. The judge must sign the judgment, and the clerk must enter it.

(2) *Criminal Forfeiture.* Forfeiture procedures are governed by Rule 32.2.

## Rule 32.1. Revoking or Modifying Probation or Supervised Release

(a) **Initial Appearance.**

(1) *Person In Custody.* A person held in custody for violating probation or supervised release

must be taken without unnecessary delay before a magistrate judge.

(A) If the person is held in custody in the district where an alleged violation occurred, the initial appearance must be in that district.

(B) If the person is held in custody in a district other than where an alleged violation occurred, the initial appearance must be in that district, or in an adjacent district if the appearance can occur more promptly there.

(2) *Upon a Summons.* When a person appears in response to a summons for violating probation or supervised release, a magistrate judge must proceed under this rule.

(3) *Advice.* The judge must inform the person of the following:

(A) the alleged violation of probation or supervised release;

(B) the person's right to retain counsel or to request that counsel be appointed if the person cannot obtain counsel; and

(C) the person's right, if held in custody, to a preliminary hearing under Rule 32.1(b)(1).

(4) *Appearance in the District with Jurisdiction.* If the person is arrested or appears in the district that has jurisdiction to conduct a

revocation hearing—either originally or by transfer of jurisdiction—the court must proceed under Rule 32.1(b)–(e).

(5) *Appearance in a District Lacking Jurisdiction.* If the person is arrested or appears in a district that does not have jurisdiction to conduct a revocation hearing, the magistrate judge must:

(A) if the alleged violation occurred in the district of arrest, conduct a preliminary hearing under Rule 32.1(b) and either:

(i) transfer the person to the district that has jurisdiction, if the judge finds probable cause to believe that a violation occurred; or

(ii) dismiss the proceedings and so notify the court that has jurisdiction, if the judge finds no probable cause to believe that a violation occurred; or

(B) if the alleged violation did not occur in the district of arrest, transfer the person to the district that has jurisdiction if:

(i) the government produces certified copies of the judgment, warrant, and warrant application, or produces copies of those certified documents by reliable electronic means; and

(ii) the judge finds that the person is the same person named in the warrant.

(6) *Release or Detention.* The magistrate judge may release or detain the person under 18 U.S.C. § 3143(a)(1) pending further proceedings. The burden of establishing by clear and convincing evidence that the person will not flee or pose a danger to any other person or to the community rests with the person.

(b) **Revocation.**

(1) *Preliminary Hearing.*

(A) *In General.* If a person is in custody for violating a condition of probation or supervised release, a magistrate judge must promptly conduct a hearing to determine whether there is probable cause to believe that a violation occurred. The person may waive the hearing.

(B) *Requirements.* The hearing must be recorded by a court reporter or by a suitable recording device. The judge must give the person:

(i) notice of the hearing and its purpose, the alleged violation, and the person's right to retain counsel or to request that counsel be appointed if the person cannot obtain counsel;

(ii) an opportunity to appear at the hearing and present evidence; and

(iii) upon request, an opportunity to question any adverse witness, unless the judge determines that the interest of justice does not require the witness to appear.

(C) *Referral.* If the judge finds probable cause, the judge must conduct a revocation hearing. If the judge does not find probable cause, the judge must dismiss the proceeding.

(2) *Revocation Hearing.* Unless waived by the person, the court must hold the revocation hearing within a reasonable time in the district having jurisdiction. The person is entitled to:

(A) written notice of the alleged violation;

(B) disclosure of the evidence against the person;

(C) an opportunity to appear, present evidence, and question any adverse witness unless the court determines that the interest of justice does not require the witness to appear;

(D) notice of the person's right to retain counsel or to request that counsel be appointed if the person cannot obtain counsel;

(E) an opportunity to make a statement and present any information in mitigation.

(c) **Modification.**

(1) *In General.* Before modifying the conditions of probation or supervised release, the court must hold a hearing, at which the person has the right to counsel and an opportunity to make a statement and present any information in mitigation.

(2) *Exceptions.* A hearing is not required if:

(A) the person waives the hearing; or

(B) the relief sought is favorable to the person and does not extend the term of probation or of supervised release; and

(C) an attorney for the government has received notice of the relief sought, has had a reasonable opportunity to object, and has not done so.

(d) **Disposition of the Case.** The court's disposition of the case is governed by 18 U.S.C. § 3563 and § 3565 (probation) and § 3583 (supervised release).

(e) **Producing a Statement.** Rule 26.2(a)–(d) and (f) applies at a hearing under this rule. If a party fails to comply with a Rule 26.2 order to produce a witness's statement, the court must not consider that witness's testimony.

## Rule 32.2. Criminal Forfeiture

(a) **Notice to the Defendant.** A court must not enter a judgment of forfeiture in a criminal proceeding unless the indictment or information contains notice to the defendant that the government will seek the forfeiture of property as part of any sentence in accordance with the applicable statute. The notice should not be designated as a count of the indictment or information. The indictment or information need not identify the property subject to forfeiture or specify the amount of any forfeiture money judgment that the government seeks.

(b) **Entering a Preliminary Order of Forfeiture.**

(1) *Forfeiture Phase of the Trial.*

(A) *Forfeiture Determinations.* As soon as practical after a verdict or finding of guilty, or after a plea of guilty or nolo contendere is accepted, on any count in an indictment or information regarding which criminal forfeiture is sought, the court must determine what property is subject to forfeiture under the applicable statute. If the government seeks forfeiture of specific property, the court must determine whether the government has established the requisite nexus between the property and the offense. If the government seeks a personal money judgment, the court must determine the amount of money that the defendant will be ordered to pay.

**(B)** *Evidence and Hearing.* The court's determination may be based on evidence already in the record, including any written plea agreement, and on any additional evidence or information submitted by the parties and accepted by the court as relevant and reliable. If the forfeiture is contested, on either party's request the court must conduct a hearing after the verdict or finding of guilty.

**(2)** *Preliminary Order.*

**(A)** *Contents of a Specific Order.* If the court finds that property is subject to forfeiture, it must promptly enter a preliminary order of forfeiture setting forth the amount of any money judgment, directing the forfeiture of specific property, and directing the forfeiture of any substitute property if the government has met the statutory criteria. The court must enter the order without regard to any third party's interest in the property. Determining whether a third party has such an interest must be deferred until any third party files a claim in an ancillary proceeding under Rule 32.2(c).

**(B)** *Timing.* Unless doing so is impractical, the court must enter the preliminary order sufficiently in advance of sentencing to allow the parties to suggest revisions or modifications before the order becomes final as to the defendant under Rule 32.2(b)(4).

**(C)** *General Order.* If, before sentencing, the court cannot identify all the specific property subject to forfeiture or calculate the total amount of the money judgment, the court may enter a forfeiture order that:

(i) lists any identified property;

(ii) describes other property in general terms; and

(iii) states that the order will be amended under Rule 32.2(e)(1) when additional specific property is identified or the amount of the money judgment has been calculated.

**(3)** *Seizing Property.* The entry of a preliminary order of forfeiture authorizes the Attorney General (or a designee) to seize the specific property subject to forfeiture; to conduct any discovery the court considers proper in identifying, locating, or disposing of the property; and to commence proceedings that comply with any statutes governing third-party rights. The court may include in the order of forfeiture conditions reasonably necessary to preserve the property's value pending any appeal.

**(4)** *Sentence and Judgment.*

**(A)** *When Final.* At sentencing—or at any time before sentencing if the defendant consents—the preliminary forfeiture order becomes final as to the defendant. If the order directs the defendant to forfeit specific property, it remains preliminary as to third parties until the ancillary proceeding is concluded under Rule 32.2(c).

**(B)** *Notice and Inclusion in the Judgment.* The court must include the forfeiture when orally announcing the sentence or must otherwise ensure that the defendant knows of the forfeiture at sentencing. The court must also include the forfeiture order, directly or by reference, in the judgment, but the court's failure to do so may be corrected at any time under Rule 36.

**(C)** *Time to Appeal.* The time for the defendant or the government to file an appeal from the forfeiture order, or from the court's failure to enter an order, begins to run when judgment is entered. If the court later amends or declines to amend a forfeiture order to include additional property under Rule 32.2(e), the defendant or the government may file an appeal regarding that property under Federal Rule of Appellate Procedure 4(b). The time for that appeal runs from the date when the order granting or denying the amendment becomes final.

(5) *Jury Determination.*

(A) *Retaining the Jury.* In any case tried before a jury, if the indictment or information states that the government is seeking forfeiture, the court must determine before the jury begins deliberating whether either party requests that the jury be retained to determine the forfeitability of specific property if it returns a guilty verdict.

(B) *Special Verdict Form.* If a party timely requests to have the jury determine forfeiture, the government must submit a proposed Special Verdict Form listing each property subject to forfeiture and asking the jury to determine whether the government has established the requisite nexus between the property and the offense committed by the defendant.

(6) *Notice of the Forfeiture Order.*

(A) *Publishing and Sending Notice.* If the court orders the forfeiture of specific property, the government must publish notice of the order and send notice to any person who reasonably appears to be a potential claimant with standing to contest the forfeiture in the ancillary proceeding.

**(B)** *Content of the Notice.* The notice must describe the forfeited property, state the times under the applicable statute when a petition contesting the forfeiture must be filed, and state the name and contact information for the government attorney to be served with the petition.

**(C)** *Means of Publication; Exceptions to Publication Requirement.* Publication must take place as described in Supplemental Rule G(4)(a)(iii) of the Federal Rules of Civil Procedure, and may be by any means described in Supplemental Rule G(4)(a)(iv). Publication is unnecessary if any exception in Supplemental Rule G(4)(a)(i) applies.

**(D)** *Means of Sending the Notice.* The notice may be sent in accordance with Supplemental Rules G(4)(b)(iii)–(v) of the Federal Rules of Civil Procedure.

**(7)** *Interlocutory Sale.* At any time before entry of a final forfeiture order, the court, in accordance with Supplemental Rule G(7) of the Federal Rules of Civil Procedure, may order the interlocutory sale of property alleged to be forfeitable.

**(c) Ancillary Proceeding; Entering a Final Order of Forfeiture.**

**(1)** *In General.* If, as prescribed by statute, a third party files a petition asserting an interest in the property to be forfeited, the court must conduct an ancillary proceeding, but no ancillary proceeding is required to the extent that the forfeiture consists of a money judgment.

(A) In the ancillary proceeding, the court may, on motion, dismiss the petition for lack of standing, for failure to state a claim, or for any other lawful reason. For purposes of the motion, the facts set forth in the petition are assumed to be true.

(B) After disposing of any motion filed under Rule 32.2(c)(1)(A) and before conducting a hearing on the petition, the court may permit the parties to conduct discovery in accordance with the Federal Rules of Civil Procedure if the court determines that discovery is necessary or desirable to resolve factual issues. When discovery ends, a party may move for summary judgment under Federal Rule of Civil Procedure 56.

(2) *Entering a Final Order.* When the ancillary proceeding ends, the court must enter a final order of forfeiture by amending the preliminary order as necessary to account for any third-party rights. If no third party files a timely petition, the preliminary order becomes the final order of forfeiture if the court finds that the defendant (or any combination of defendants convicted in the case) had an interest in the property that is forfeitable under the applicable statute. The defendant may not object to the entry of the final order on the ground that the property belongs, in whole or in part, to a codefendant or third party; nor may a third party object to the final order on the ground that the third party had an interest in the property.

(3) *Multiple Petitions.* If multiple third-party petitions are filed in the same case, an order dismissing or granting one petition is not appealable until rulings are made on all the petitions, unless the court determines that there is no just reason for delay.

(4) *Ancillary Proceeding Not Part of Sentencing.* An ancillary proceeding is not part of sentencing.

(d) **Stay Pending Appeal.** If a defendant appeals from a conviction or an order of forfeiture, the court may stay the order of forfeiture on terms appropriate to ensure that the property remains available pending appellate review. A stay does not delay the ancillary proceeding or the determination of a third party's rights or interests. If the court rules in favor of any third party while an appeal is pending, the court may amend the order of forfeiture but must not transfer any property interest to a third party until the decision on appeal becomes final, unless the defendant consents in writing or on the record.

(e) **Subsequently Located Property; Substitute Property.**

(1) *In General.* On the government's motion, the court may at any time enter an order of forfeiture or amend an existing order of forfeiture to include property that:

(A) is subject to forfeiture under an existing order of forfeiture but was located and identified after that order was entered; or

(B) is substitute property that qualifies for forfeiture under an applicable statute.

**(2)** *Procedure.* If the government shows that the property is subject to forfeiture under Rule 32.2(e)(1), the court must:

**(A)** enter an order forfeiting that property, or amend an existing preliminary or final order to include it; and

**(B)** if a third party files a petition claiming an interest in the property, conduct an ancillary proceeding under Rule 32.2(c).

**(3)** *Jury Trial Limited.* There is no right to a jury trial under Rule 32.2(e).

## Rule 33.  New Trial

**(a)  Defendant's Motion.** Upon the defendant's motion, the court may vacate any judgment and grant a new trial if the interest of justice so requires. If the case was tried without a jury, the court may take additional testimony and enter a new judgment.

**(b)  Time to File.**

**(1)** *Newly Discovered Evidence.* Any motion for a new trial grounded on newly discovered evidence must be filed within 3 years after the verdict or finding of guilty. If an appeal is pending, the court may not grant a motion for a new trial until the appellate court remands the case.

**(2)** *Other Grounds.* Any motion for a new trial grounded on any reason other than newly discovered evidence must be filed within 14 days after the verdict or finding of guilty.

## Rule 34. Arresting Judgment

(a) **In General.** Upon the defendant's motion or on its own, the court must arrest judgment if the court does not have jurisdiction of the charged offense.

(b) **Time to File.** The defendant must move to arrest judgment within 14 days after the court accepts a verdict or finding of guilty, or after a plea of guilty or nolo contendere.

## Rule 35. Correcting or Reducing a Sentence

(a) **Correcting Clear Error.** Within 14 days after sentencing, the court may correct a sentence that resulted from arithmetical, technical, or other clear error.

(b) **Reducing a Sentence for Substantial Assistance.**

(1) *In General.* Upon the government's motion made within one year of sentencing, the court may reduce a sentence if the defendant, after sentencing, provided substantial assistance in investigating or prosecuting another person.

(2) *Later Motion.* Upon the government's motion made more than one year after sentencing, the court may reduce a sentence if the defendant's substantial assistance involved:

(A) information not known to the defendant until one year or more after sentencing;

(B) information provided by the defendant to the government within one year of sentencing, but which did not become useful to the government until more than one year after sentencing; or

(C) information the usefulness of which could not reasonably have been anticipated by the defendant until more than one year after sentencing and which was promptly provided to the government after its usefulness was reasonably apparent to the defendant.

(3) *Evaluating Substantial Assistance.* In evaluating whether the defendant has provided substantial assistance, the court may consider the defendant's presentence assistance.

(4) *Below Statutory Minimum.* When acting under Rule 35(b), the court may reduce the sentence to a level below the minimum sentence established by statute.

(c) **"Sentencing" Defined.** As used in this rule, "sentencing" means the oral announcement of the sentence.

## Rule 36.   Clerical Error

After giving any notice it considers appropriate, the court may at any time correct a clerical error in a judgment, order, or other part of the record, or correct an error in the record arising from oversight or omission.

## Rule 37.   Indicative Ruling on a Motion for Relief That Is Barred by a Pending Appeal

(a) **Relief Pending Appeal.** If a timely motion is made for relief that the court lacks authority to grant because of an appeal that has been docketed and is pending, the court may:

   (1)  defer considering the motion;

   (2)  deny the motion; or

   (3)  state either that it would grant the motion if the court of appeals remands for that purpose or that the motion raises a substantial issue.

(b) **Notice to the Court of Appeals.** The movant must promptly notify the circuit clerk under Federal Rule of Appellate Procedure 12.1 if the district court states that it would grant the motion or that the motion raises a substantial issue.

(c) **Remand.** The district court may decide the motion if the court of appeals remands for that purpose.

## Rule 38.   Staying a Sentence or a Disability

(a) **Death Sentence.** The court must stay a death sentence if the defendant appeals the conviction or sentence.

(b) **Imprisonment.**

(1) *Stay Granted.* If the defendant is released pending appeal, the court must stay a sentence of imprisonment.

(2) *Stay Denied; Place of Confinement.* If the defendant is not released pending appeal, the court may recommend to the Attorney General that the defendant be confined near the place of the trial or appeal for a period reasonably necessary to permit the defendant to assist in preparing the appeal.

(c) **Fine.** If the defendant appeals, the district court, or the court of appeals under Federal Rule of Appellate Procedure 8, may stay a sentence to pay a fine or a fine and costs. The court may stay the sentence on any terms considered appropriate and may require the defendant to:

(1) deposit all or part of the fine and costs into the district court's registry pending appeal;

(2) post a bond to pay the fine and costs; or

(3) submit to an examination concerning the defendant's assets and, if appropriate, order the defendant to refrain from dissipating assets.

**(d) Probation.** If the defendant appeals, the court may stay a sentence of probation. The court must set the terms of any stay.

**(e) Restitution and Notice to Victims.**

(1) *In General.* If the defendant appeals, the district court, or the court of appeals under Federal Rule of Appellate Procedure 8, may stay—on any terms considered appropriate—any sentence providing for restitution under 18 U.S.C. § 3556 or notice under 18 U.S.C. § 3555.

(2) *Ensuring Compliance.* The court may issue any order reasonably necessary to ensure compliance with a restitution order or a notice order after disposition of an appeal, including:

(A) a restraining order;

(B) an injunction;

(C) an order requiring the defendant to deposit all or part of any monetary restitution into the district court's registry; or

(D) an order requiring the defendant to post a bond.

**(f) Forfeiture.** A stay of a forfeiture order is governed by Rule 32.2(d).

**(g) Disability.** If the defendant's conviction or sentence creates a civil or employment disability under federal law, the district court, or the court of appeals under Federal Rule of Appellate Procedure 8, may stay the disability pending appeal on any terms considered appropriate. The court may issue any order reasonably necessary to protect the interest represented by the disability pending appeal, including a restraining order or an injunction.

## Rule 39.   [Reserved]

# TITLE VIII. SUPPLEMENTARY AND SPECIAL PROCEEDINGS

## Rule 40. Arrest for Failing to Appear in Another District or for Violating Conditions of Release Set in Another District

(a) **In General.** A person must be taken without unnecessary delay before a magistrate judge in the district of arrest if the person has been arrested under a warrant issued in another district for:

    (i) failing to appear as required by the terms of that person's release under 18 U.S.C. §§ 3141–3156 or by a subpoena; or

    (ii) violating conditions of release set in another district.

(b) **Proceedings.** The judge must proceed under Rule 5(c)(3) as applicable.

(c) **Release or Detention Order.** The judge may modify any previous release or detention order issued in another district, but must state in writing the reasons for doing so.

(d) **Video Teleconferencing.** If the defendant consents, video teleconferencing may be used to conduct an appearance under this rule if the defendant consents.

## Rule 41.   Search and Seizure

(a) Scope and Definitions.

(1) *Scope.* This rule does not modify any statute regulating search or seizure, or the issuance and execution of a search warrant in special circumstances.

(2) *Definitions.* The following definitions apply under this rule:

(A) "Property" includes documents, books, papers, any other tangible objects, and information.

(B) "Daytime" means the hours between 6:00 a.m. and 10:00 p.m. according to local time.

(C) "Federal law enforcement officer" means a government agent (other than an attorney for the government) who is engaged in enforcing the criminal laws and is within any category of officers authorized by the Attorney General to request a search warrant.

(D) "Domestic terrorism" and "international terrorism" have the meanings set out in 18 U.S.C. § 2331.

(E) "Tracking device" has the meaning set out in 18 U.S.C. § 3117(b).

(b) **Venue for a Warrant Application.** At the request of a federal law enforcement officer or an attorney for the government:

(1) a magistrate judge with authority in the district—or if none is reasonably available, a judge of a state court of record in the district—has authority to issue a warrant to search for and seize a person or property located within the district;

(2) a magistrate judge with authority in the district has authority to issue a warrant for a person or property outside the district if the person or property is located within the district when the warrant is issued but might move or be moved outside the district before the warrant is executed;

(3) a magistrate judge—in an investigation of domestic terrorism or international terrorism—with authority in any district in which activities related to the terrorism may have occurred has authority to issue a warrant for a person or property within or outside that district;

(4) a magistrate judge with authority in the district has authority to issue a warrant to install within the district a tracking device; the warrant may authorize use of the device to track the movement of a person or property located within the district, outside the district, or both; and

(5) a magistrate judge having authority in any district where activities related to the crime may have occurred, or in the District of Columbia, may issue a warrant for property that is located outside the jurisdiction of any state or district, but within any of the following:

(A) a United States territory, possession, or commonwealth;

(B) the premises—no matter who owns them—of a United States diplomatic or consular mission in a foreign state, including any appurtenant building, part of a building, or land used for the mission's purposes; or

(C) a residence and any appurtenant land owned or leased by the United States and used by United States personnel assigned to a United States diplomatic or consular mission in a foreign state.

(6) a magistrate judge with authority in any district where activities related to a crime may have occurred has authority to issue a warrant to use remote access to search electronic storage media and to seize or copy electronically stored information located within or outside that district if:

(A) the district where the media or information is located has been concealed through technological means; or

**(B)** in an investigation of a violation of 18 U.S.C. § 1030(a)(5), the media are protected computers that have been damaged without authorization and are located in five or more districts.

**(c) Persons or Property Subject to Search or Seizure.** A warrant may be issued for any of the following:

(1) evidence of a crime;

(2) contraband, fruits of crime, or other items illegally possessed;

(3) property designed for use, intended for use, or used in committing a crime; or

(4) a person to be arrested or a person who is unlawfully restrained.

**(d) Obtaining a Warrant.**

(1) *In General.* After receiving an affidavit or other information, a magistrate judge—or if authorized by Rule 41(b), a judge of a state court of record—must issue the warrant if there is probable cause to search for and seize a person or property or to install and use a tracking device.

(2) *Requesting a Warrant in the Presence of a Judge.*

**(A)** *Warrant on an Affidavit.* When a federal law enforcement officer or an attorney for the government presents an affidavit in support of a warrant, the judge may require the affiant to appear personally and may examine under oath the affiant and any witness the affiant produces.

**(B)** *Warrant on Sworn Testimony.* The judge may wholly or partially dispense with a written affidavit and base a warrant on sworn testimony if doing so is reasonable under the circumstances.

**(C)** *Recording Testimony.* Testimony taken in support of a warrant must be recorded by a court reporter or by a suitable recording device, and the judge must file the transcript or recording with the clerk, along with any affidavit.

**(3)** ***Requesting a Warrant by Telephonic or Other Means.*** In accordance with Rule 4.1, a magistrate judge may issue a warrant based on information communicated by telephone or other reliable electronic means.

**(e) Issuing the Warrant.**

**(1)** *In General.* The magistrate judge or a judge of a state court of record must issue the warrant to an officer authorized to execute it.

### (2) *Contents of the Warrant.*

(A) *Warrant to Search for and Seize a Person or Property.* Except for a tracking-device warrant, the warrant must identify the person or property to be searched, identify any person or property to be seized, and designate the magistrate judge to whom it must be returned. The warrant must command the officer to:

(i) execute the warrant within a specified time no longer than 14 days;

(ii) execute the warrant during the daytime, unless the judge for good cause expressly authorizes execution at another time; and

(iii) return the warrant to the magistrate judge designated in the warrant.

(B) *Warrant Seeking Electronically Stored Information.* A warrant under Rule 41(e)(2)(A) may authorize the seizure of electronic storage media or the seizure or copying of electronically stored information. Unless otherwise specified, the warrant authorizes a later review of the media or information consistent with the warrant. The time for executing the warrant in Rule 41(e)(2)(A) and (f)(1)(A) refers to the seizure or on-site copying of the media or information, and not to any later off-site copying or review.

**(C)** *Warrant for a Tracking Device.* A tracking-device warrant must identify the person or property to be tracked, designate the magistrate judge to whom it must be returned, and specify a reasonable length of time that the device may be used. The time must not exceed 45 days from the date the warrant was issued. The court may, for good cause, grant one or more extensions for a reasonable period not to exceed 45 days each. The warrant must command the officer to:

(i) complete any installation authorized by the warrant within a specified time no longer than 10 calendar days;

(ii) perform any installation authorized by the warrant during the daytime, unless the judge for good cause expressly authorizes installation at another time; and

(iii) return the warrant to the judge designated in the warrant.

**(f) Executing and Returning the Warrant.**

(1) *Warrant to Search for and Seize a Person or Property.*

**(A)** *Noting the Time.* The officer executing the warrant must enter on it the exact date and time it was executed.

**(B)** *Inventory.* An officer present during the execution of the warrant must prepare and verify an inventory of any property seized. The officer must do so in the presence of another officer and the person from whom, or from whose premises, the property was taken. If either one is not present, the officer must prepare and verify the inventory in the presence of at least one other credible person. In a case involving the seizure of electronic storage media or the seizure or copying of electronically stored information, the inventory may be limited to describing the physical storage media that were seized or copied. The officer may retain a copy of the electronically stored information that was seized or copied.

**(C)** *Receipt.* The officer executing the warrant must give a copy of the warrant and a receipt for the property taken to the person from whom, or from whose premises, the property was taken or leave a copy of the warrant and receipt at the place where the officer took the property. For a warrant to use remote access to search electronic storage media and seize or copy electronically stored information, the officer must make reasonable efforts to serve a copy of the warrant and receipt on the person whose property was searched or who possessed the information that was seized or copied. Service may be accomplished by any means, including electronic means, reasonably calculated to reach that person.

**(D)** *Return.* The officer executing the warrant must promptly return it—together with a copy of the inventory—to the magistrate judge designated on the warrant. The officer may do so by reliable electronic means. The judge must, on request, give a copy of the inventory to the person from whom, or from whose premises, the property was taken and to the applicant for the warrant.

(2) *Warrant for a Tracking Device.*

**(A)** *Noting the Time.* The officer executing a tracking-device warrant must enter on it the exact date and time the device was installed and the period during which it was used.

**(B)** *Return.* Within 10 calendar days after the use of the tracking device has ended, the officer executing the warrant must return it to the judge designated in the warrant. The officer may do so by reliable electronic means.

**(C)** *Service.* Within 10 calendar days after the use of the tracking device has ended, the officer executing a tracking-device warrant must serve a copy of the warrant on the person who was tracked or whose property was tracked. Service may be accomplished by delivering a copy to the person who, or whose property, was tracked; or by leaving a copy at the person's residence or usual place of abode with an individual of suitable age and discretion who resides at that location and by mailing a copy to the person's last known address. Upon request of the government, the judge may delay notice as provided in Rule 41(f)(3).

(3) *Delayed Notice.* Upon the government's request, a magistrate judge—or if authorized by Rule 41(b), a judge of a state court of record—may delay any notice required by this rule if the delay is authorized by statute.

(g) **Motion to Return Property.** A person aggrieved by an unlawful search and seizure of property or by the deprivation of property may move for the property's return. The motion must be filed in the district where the property was seized. The court must receive evidence on any factual issue necessary to decide the motion. If it grants the motion, the court must return the property to the movant, but may impose reasonable conditions to protect access to the property and its use in later proceedings.

**(h) Motion to Suppress.** A defendant may move to suppress evidence in the court where the trial will occur, as Rule 12 provides.

**(i) Forwarding Papers to the Clerk.** The magistrate judge to whom the warrant is returned must attach to the warrant a copy of the return, of the inventory, and of all other related papers and must deliver them to the clerk in the district where the property was seized.

## Rule 42.  Criminal Contempt

**(a) Disposition After Notice.** Any person who commits criminal contempt may be punished for that contempt after prosecution on notice.

   **(1)** *Notice.* The court must give the person notice in open court, in an order to show cause, or in an arrest order. The notice must:

   **(A)** state the time and place of the trial;

   **(B)** allow the defendant a reasonable time to prepare a defense; and

   **(C)** state the essential facts constituting the charged criminal contempt and describe it as such.

   **(2)** *Appointing a Prosecutor.* The court must request that the contempt be prosecuted by an attorney for the government, unless the interest of justice requires the appointment of another attorney. If the government declines the request, the court must appoint another attorney to prosecute the contempt.

(3) *Trial and Disposition.* A person being prosecuted for criminal contempt is entitled to a jury trial in any case in which federal law so provides and must be released or detained as Rule 46 provides. If the criminal contempt involves disrespect toward or criticism of a judge, that judge is disqualified from presiding at the contempt trial or hearing unless the defendant consents. Upon a finding or verdict of guilty, the court must impose the punishment.

(b) **Summary Disposition.** Notwithstanding any other provision of these rules, the court (other than a magistrate judge) may summarily punish a person who commits criminal contempt in its presence if the judge saw or heard the contemptuous conduct and so certifies; a magistrate judge may summarily punish a person as provided in 28 U.S.C. § 636(e). The contempt order must recite the facts, be signed by the judge, and be filed with the clerk.

# TITLE IX.  GENERAL PROVISIONS

## Rule 43.  Defendant's Presence

(a) **When Required.** Unless this rule, Rule 5, or Rule 10 provides otherwise, the defendant must be present at:

(1) the initial appearance, the initial arraignment, and the plea;

(2) every trial stage, including jury impanelment and the return of the verdict; and

(3) sentencing.

(b) **When Not Required.** A defendant need not be present under any of the following circumstances:

(1) *Organizational Defendant.* The defendant is an organization represented by counsel who is present.

(2) *Misdemeanor Offense.* The offense is punishable by fine or by imprisonment for not more than one year, or both, and with the defendant's written consent, the court permits arraignment, plea, trial, and sentencing to occur by video teleconferencing or in the defendant's absence.

(3) *Conference or Hearing on a Legal Question.* The proceeding involves only a conference or hearing on a question of law.

(4) **Sentence Correction.** The proceeding involves the correction or reduction of sentence under Rule 35 or 18 U.S.C. § 3582(c).

(c) **Waiving Continued Presence.**

(1) *In General.* A defendant who was initially present at trial, or who had pleaded guilty or nolo contendere, waives the right to be present under the following circumstances:

(A) when the defendant is voluntarily absent after the trial has begun, regardless of whether the court informed the defendant of an obligation to remain during trial;

(B) in a noncapital case, when the defendant is voluntarily absent during sentencing; or

(C) when the court warns the defendant that it will remove the defendant from the courtroom for disruptive behavior, but the defendant persists in conduct that justifies removal from the courtroom.

(2) *Waiver's Effect.* If the defendant waives the right to be present, the trial may proceed to completion, including the verdict's return and sentencing, during the defendant's absence.

# Rule 44. Right to and Appointment of Counsel

(a) **Right to Appointed Counsel.** A defendant who is unable to obtain counsel is entitled to have counsel appointed to represent the defendant at every stage of the proceeding from initial appearance through appeal, unless the defendant waives this right.

(b) **Appointment Procedure.** Federal law and local court rules govern the procedure for implementing the right to counsel.

(c) **Inquiry Into Joint Representation.**

(1) *Joint Representation.* Joint representation occurs when:

(A) two or more defendants have been charged jointly under Rule 8(b) or have been joined for trial under Rule 13; and

(B) the defendants are represented by the same counsel, or counsel who are associated in law practice.

(2) *Court's Responsibilities in Cases of Joint Representation.* The court must promptly inquire about the propriety of joint representation and must personally advise each defendant of the right to the effective assistance of counsel, including separate representation. Unless there is good cause to believe that no conflict of interest

is likely to arise, the court must take appropriate measures to protect each defendant's right to counsel.

## Rule 45. Computing and Extending Time

**(a) Computing Time.** The following rules apply in computing any period of time specified in these rules, in any local rule or court order, or in any statute that does not specify a method of computing time.

(1) *Period Stated in Days or a Longer Unit.* When the period is stated in days or a longer unit of time:

(**A**) exclude the day of the event that triggers the period;

(**B**) count every day, including intermediate Saturdays, Sundays, and legal holidays; and

(**C**) include the last day of the period, but if the last day is a Saturday, Sunday, or legal holiday, the period continues to run until the end of the next day that is not a Saturday, Sunday, or legal holiday.

(2) *Period Stated in Hours.* When the period is stated in hours:

(**A**) begin counting immediately on the occurrence of the event that triggers the period;

**(B)** count every hour, including hours during intermediate Saturdays, Sundays, and legal holidays; and

**(C)** if the period would end on a Saturday, Sunday, or legal holiday, the period continues to run until the same time on the next day that is not a Saturday, Sunday, or legal holiday.

**(3)** *Inaccessibility of the Clerk's Office.* Unless the court orders otherwise, if the clerk's office is inaccessible:

**(A)** on the last day for filing under Rule 45(a) (1), then the time for filing is extended to the first accessible day that is not a Saturday, Sunday, or legal holiday; or

**(B)** during the last hour for filing under Rule 45(a)(2), then the time for filing is extended to the same time on the first accessible day that is not a Saturday, Sunday, or legal holiday.

**(4)** *"Last Day" Defined.* Unless a different time is set by a statute, local rule, or court order, the last day ends:

**(A)** for electronic filing, at midnight in the court's time zone; and

**(B)** for filing by other means, when the clerk's office is scheduled to close.

(5) *"Next Day" Defined.* The "next day" is determined by continuing to count forward when the period is measured after an event and backward when measured before an event.

(6) *"Legal Holiday" Defined.* "Legal holiday" means:

(A) the day set aside by statute for observing New Year's Day, Martin Luther King Jr.'s Birthday, Washington's Birthday, Memorial Day, Independence Day, Labor Day, Columbus Day, Veterans' Day, Thanksgiving Day, or Christmas Day;

(B) any day declared a holiday by the President or Congress; and

(C) for periods that are measured after an event, any other day declared a holiday by the state where the district court is located.

(b) **Extending Time.**

(1) *In General.* When an act must or may be done within a specified period, the court on its own may extend the time, or for good cause may do so on a party's motion made:

(A) before the originally prescribed or previously extended time expires; or

(B) after the time expires if the party failed to act because of excusable neglect.

(2) *Exception.* The court may not extend the time to take any action under Rule 35, except as stated in that rule.

(c) **Additional Time After Certain Kinds of Service.** Whenever a party must or may act within a specified time after being served and service is made under Rule 49(a)(4)(C), (D), and (E), 3 days are added after the period would otherwise expire under subdivision (a).

## Rule 46. Release from Custody; Supervising Detention

(a) **Before Trial.** The provisions of 18 U.S.C. §§ 3142 and 3144 govern pretrial release.

(b) **During Trial.** A person released before trial continues on release during trial under the same terms and conditions. But the court may order different terms and conditions or terminate the release if necessary to ensure that the person will be present during trial or that the person's conduct will not obstruct the orderly and expeditious progress of the trial.

(c) **Pending Sentencing or Appeal.** The provisions of 18 U.S.C. § 3143 govern release pending sentencing or appeal. The burden of establishing that the defendant will not flee or pose a danger to any other person or to the community rests with the defendant.

(d) **Pending Hearing on a Violation of Probation or Supervised Release.** Rule 32.1(a)(6) governs release pending a hearing on a violation of probation or supervised release.

(e) **Surety.** The court must not approve a bond unless any surety appears to be qualified. Every surety, except a legally approved corporate surety, must demonstrate by affidavit that its assets are adequate. The court may require the affidavit to describe the following:

(1) the property that the surety proposes to use as security;

(2) any encumbrance on that property;

(3) the number and amount of any other undischarged bonds and bail undertakings the surety has issued; and

(4) any other liability of the surety.

(f) **Bail Forfeiture.**

(1) *Declaration.* The court must declare the bail forfeited if a condition of the bond is breached.

(2) *Setting Aside.* The court may set aside in whole or in part a bail forfeiture upon any condition the court may impose if:

**(A)** the surety later surrenders into custody the person released on the surety's appearance bond; or

**(B)** it appears that justice does not require bail forfeiture.

**(3)** *Enforcement.*

**(A)** *Default Judgment and Execution.* If it does not set aside a bail forfeiture, the court must, upon the government's motion, enter a default judgment.

**(B)** *Jurisdiction and Service.* By entering into a bond, each surety submits to the district court's jurisdiction and irrevocably appoints the district clerk as its agent to receive service of any filings affecting its liability.

**(C)** *Motion to Enforce.* The court may, upon the government's motion, enforce the surety's liability without an independent action. The government must serve any motion, and notice as the court prescribes, on the district clerk. If so served, the clerk must promptly mail a copy to the surety at its last known address.

**(4)** *Remission.* After entering a judgment under Rule 46(f)(3), the court may remit in whole or in part the judgment under the same conditions specified in Rule 46(f)(2).

**(g) Exoneration.** The court must exonerate the surety and release any bail when a bond condition has been satisfied or when the court has set aside or remitted the forfeiture. The court must exonerate a surety who deposits cash in the amount of the bond or timely surrenders the defendant into custody.

**(h) Supervising Detention Pending Trial.**

(1) *In General.* To eliminate unnecessary detention, the court must supervise the detention within the district of any defendants awaiting trial and of any persons held as material witnesses.

(2) *Reports.* An attorney for the government must report biweekly to the court, listing each material witness held in custody for more than 10 days pending indictment, arraignment, or trial. For each material witness listed in the report, an attorney for the government must state why the witness should not be released with or without a deposition being taken under Rule 15(a).

**(i) Forfeiture of Property.** The court may dispose of a charged offense by ordering the forfeiture of 18 U.S.C. § 3142(c)(1)(B)(xi) property under 18 U.S.C. § 3146(d), if a fine in the amount of the property's value would be an appropriate sentence for the charged offense.

(j) **Producing a Statement.**

(1) *In General.* Rule 26.2(a)–(d) and (f) applies at a detention hearing under 18 U.S.C. § 3142, unless the court for good cause rules otherwise.

(2) *Sanctions for Not Producing a Statement.* If a party disobeys a Rule 26.2 order to produce a witness's statement, the court must not consider that witness's testimony at the detention hearing.

## Rule 47. Motions and Supporting Affidavits

(a) **In General.** A party applying to the court for an order must do so by motion.

(b) **Form and Content of a Motion.** A motion—except when made during a trial or hearing—must be in writing, unless the court permits the party to make the motion by other means. A motion must state the grounds on which it is based and the relief or order sought. A motion may be supported by affidavit.

(c) **Timing of a Motion.** A party must serve a written motion—other than one that the court may hear ex parte—and any hearing notice at least 7 days before the hearing date, unless a rule or court order sets a different period. For good cause, the court may set a different period upon ex parte application.

(d) **Affidavit Supporting a Motion.** The moving party must serve any supporting affidavit with the motion. A responding party must serve any opposing affidavit at least one day before the hearing, unless the court permits later service.

## Rule 48.   Dismissal

(a) **By the Government.** The government may, with leave of court, dismiss an indictment, information, or complaint. The government may not dismiss the prosecution during trial without the defendant's consent.

(b) **By the Court.** The court may dismiss an indictment, information, or complaint if unnecessary delay occurs in:

    (1)  presenting a charge to a grand jury;

    (2)  filing an information against a defendant; or

    (3)  bringing a defendant to trial.

## Rule 49.   Serving and Filing Papers

(a)  Service on a Party.

    (1)  *What is Required.* Each of the following must be served on every party: any written motion (other than one to be heard ex parte), written notice, designation of the record on appeal, or similar paper.

**(2)** *Serving a Party's Attorney.* Unless the court orders otherwise, when these rules or a court order requires or permits service on a party represented by an attorney, service must be made on the attorney instead of the party.

**(3)** *Service by Electronic Means.*

(A) *Using the Court's Electronic-Filing System.* A party represented by an attorney may serve a paper on a registered user by filing it with the court's electronic-filing system. A party not represented by an attorney may do so only if allowed by court order or local rule. Service is complete upon filing, but is not effective if the serving party learns that it did not reach the person to be served.

(B) *Using Other Electronic Means.* A paper may be served by any other electronic means that the person consented to in writing. Service is complete upon transmission, but is not effective if the serving party learns that it did not reach the person to be served.

**(4)** *Service by Nonelectronic Means.* A paper may be served by:

(A) handing it to the person;

(B) leaving it:

         (i)  at the person's office with a clerk or other person in charge or, if no one is in charge, in a conspicuous place in the office; or

         (ii)  if the person has no office or the office is closed, at the person's dwelling or usual place of abode with someone of suitable age and discretion who resides there;

     (C)  mailing it to the person's last known address—in which event service is complete upon mailing;

     (D)  leaving it with the court clerk if the person has no known address; or

     (E)  delivering it by any other means that the person consented to in writing—in which event service is complete when the person making service delivers it to the agency designated to make delivery.

  **(b)  Filing.**

   (1)  *When Required; Certificate of Service.* Any paper that is required to be served must be filed no later than a reasonable time after service. No certificate of service is required when a paper is served by filing it with the court's electronic-filing system. When a paper is served by other means, a certificate of service must be filed with it or within a reasonable time after service or filing.

**(2)** *Means of Filing.*

(A) *Electronically.* A paper is filed electronically by filing it with the court's electronic-filing system. A filing made through a person's electronic-filing account and authorized by that person, together with the person's name on a signature block, constitutes the person's signature. A paper filed electronically is written or in writing under these rules.

(B) *Nonelectronically.* A paper not filed electronically is filed by delivering it:

(i) to the clerk; or

(ii) to a judge who agrees to accept it for filing, and who must then note the filing date on the paper and promptly send it to the clerk.

**(3)** *Means Used by Represented and Unrepresented Parties.*

(A) *Represented Party.* A party represented by an attorney must file electronically, unless nonelectronic filing is allowed by the court for good cause or is allowed or required by local rule.

(B) *Unrepresented Party.* A party not represented by an attorney must file nonelectronically, unless allowed to file electronically by court order or local rule.

(4) *Signature.* Every written motion and other paper must be signed by at least one attorney of record in the attorney's name—or by a person filing a paper if the person is not represented by an attorney. The paper must state the signer's address, e-mail address, and telephone number. Unless a rule or statute specifically states otherwise, a pleading need not be verified or accompanied by an affidavit. The court must strike an unsigned paper unless the omission is promptly corrected after being called to the attorney's or person's attention.

(5) *Acceptance by the Clerk.* The clerk must not refuse to file a paper solely because it is not in the form prescribed by these rules or by a local rule or practice.

(c) **Service and Filing by Nonparties.** A nonparty may serve and file a paper only if doing so is required or permitted by law. A nonparty must serve every party as required by Rule 49(a), but may use the court's electronic-filing system only if allowed by court order or local rule.

(d) **Notice of a Court Order.** When the court issues an order on any post-arraignment motion, the clerk must serve notice of the entry on each party as required by Rule 49(a). A party also may serve notice of the entry by the same means. Except as Federal Rule of Appellate Procedure 4(b) provides otherwise, the clerk's failure to give notice does not affect the time to appeal, or relieve—or authorize the court to relieve— a party's failure to appeal within the allowed time.

## Rule 49.1. Privacy Protection For Filings Made with the Court

(a) **Redacted Filings.** Unless the court orders otherwise, in an electronic or paper filing with the court that contains an individual's social-security number, taxpayer-identification number, or birth date, the name of an individual known to be a minor, a financial-account number, or the home address of an individual, a party or nonparty making the filing may include only:

(1) the last four digits of the social-security number and taxpayer-identification number;

(2) the year of the individual's birth;

(3) the minor's initials;

(4) the last four digits of the financial-account number; and

(5) the city and state of the home address.

(b) **Exemptions from the Redaction Requirement.**
The redaction requirement does not apply to the
following:

(1) a financial-account number or real property
address that identifies the property allegedly
subject to forfeiture in a forfeiture proceeding;

(2) the record of an administrative or agency
proceeding;

(3) the official record of a state-court proceeding;

(4) the record of a court or tribunal, if that record was not subject to the redaction requirement when originally filed;

(5) a filing covered by Rule 49.1(d);

(6) a pro se filing in an action brought under 28
U.S.C. §§ 2241, 2254, or 2255;

(7) a court filing that is related to a criminal
matter or investigation and that is prepared before the filing of a criminal charge or is not filed
as part of any docketed criminal case;

(8) an arrest or search warrant; and

(9) a charging document and an affidavit filed
in support of any charging document.

(c) **Immigration Cases.** A filing in an action
brought under 28 U.S.C. § 2241 that relates to the

petitioner's immigration rights is governed by Federal Rule of Civil Procedure 5.2.

**(d) Filings Made Under Seal.** The court may order that a filing be made under seal without redaction. The court may later unseal the filing or order the person who made the filing to file a redacted version for the public record.

**(e) Protective Orders.** For good cause, the court may by order in a case:

(1) require redaction of additional information; or

(2) limit or prohibit a nonparty's remote electronic access to a document filed with the court.

**(f) Option for Additional Unredacted Filing Under Seal.** A person making a redacted filing may also file an unredacted copy under seal. The court must retain the unredacted copy as part of the record.

**(g) Option for Filing a Reference List.** A filing that contains redacted information may be filed together with a reference list that identifies each item of redacted information and specifies an appropriate identifier that uniquely corresponds to each item listed. The list must be filed under seal and may be amended as of right. Any reference in the case to a listed identifier will be construed to refer to the corresponding item of information.

**(h) Waiver of Protection of Identifiers.** A person waives the protection of Rule 49.1(a) as to the person's own information by filing it without redaction and not under seal.

## Rule 50.  Prompt Disposition

Scheduling preference must be given to criminal proceedings as far as practicable.

## Rule 51.  Preserving Claimed Error

**(a) Exceptions Unnecessary.** Exceptions to rulings or orders of the court are unnecessary.

**(b) Preserving a Claim of Error.** A party may preserve a claim of error by informing the court—when the court ruling or order is made or sought—of the action the party wishes the court to take, or the party's objection to the court's action and the grounds for that objection. If a party does not have an opportunity to object to a ruling or order, the absence of an objection does not later prejudice that party. A ruling or order that admits or excludes evidence is governed by Federal Rule of Evidence 103.

## Rule 52.  Harmless and Plain Error

(a) **Harmless Error.** Any error, defect, irregularity, or variance that does not affect substantial rights must be disregarded.

(b) **Plain Error.** A plain error that affects substantial rights may be considered even though it was not brought to the court's attention.

## Rule 53.  Courtroom Photographing and Broadcasting Prohibited

Except as otherwise provided by a statute or these rules, the court must not permit the taking of photographs in the courtroom during judicial proceedings or the broadcasting of judicial proceedings from the courtroom.

## Rule 54.  [Transferred][1]

## Rule 55.  Records

The clerk of the district court must keep records of criminal proceedings in the form prescribed by the Director of the Administrative Office of the United States Courts. The clerk must enter in the records every court order or judgment and the date of entry.

---

1. Portions of Rule 54 were moved to Rule 1, others were deleted.

## Rule 56.  When Court Is Open

(a)  **In General.** A district court is considered always open for any filing, and for issuing and returning process, making a motion, or entering an order.

(b)  **Office Hours.** The clerk's office—with the clerk or a deputy in attendance—must be open during business hours on all days except Saturdays, Sundays, and legal holidays.

(c)  **Special Hours.** A court may provide by local rule or order that its clerk's office will be open for specified hours on Saturdays or legal holidays other than those set aside by statute for observing New Year's Day, Martin Luther King, Jr.'s Birthday, Washington's Birthday, Memorial Day, Independence Day, Labor Day, Columbus Day, Veterans' Day, Thanksgiving Day, and Christmas Day.

## Rule 57.  District Court Rules

(a)  **In General.**

(1)  *Adopting Local Rules.* Each district court acting by a majority of its district judges may, after giving appropriate public notice and an opportunity to comment, make and amend rules governing its practice. A local rule must be consistent with—but not duplicative of—federal statutes and rules adopted under 28 U.S.C.

§ 2072 and must conform to any uniform numbering system prescribed by the Judicial Conference of the United States.

**(2)** *Limiting Enforcement.* A local rule imposing a requirement of form must not be enforced in a manner that causes a party to lose rights because of an unintentional failure to comply with the requirement.

**(b) Procedure When There Is No Controlling Law.** A judge may regulate practice in any manner consistent with federal law, these rules, and the local rules of the district. No sanction or other disadvantage may be imposed for noncompliance with any requirement not in federal law, federal rules, or the local district rules unless the alleged violator was furnished with actual notice of the requirement before the noncompliance.

**(c) Effective Date and Notice.** A local rule adopted under this rule takes effect on the date specified by the district court and remains in effect unless amended by the district court or abrogated by the judicial council of the circuit in which the district is located. Copies of local rules and their amendments, when promulgated, must be furnished to the judicial council and the Administrative Office of the United States Courts and must be made available to the public.

# Rule 58. Petty Offenses and Other Misdemeanors

(a) Scope.

(1) *In General.* These rules apply in petty offense and other misdemeanor cases and on appeal to a district judge in a case tried by a magistrate judge, unless this rule provides otherwise.

(2) *Petty Offense Case Without Imprisonment.* In a case involving a petty offense for which no sentence of imprisonment will be imposed, the court may follow any provision of these rules that is not inconsistent with this rule and that the court considers appropriate.

(3) *Definition.* As used in this rule, the term "petty offense for which no sentence of imprisonment will be imposed" means a petty offense for which the court determines that, in the event of conviction, no sentence of imprisonment will be imposed.

(b) Pretrial Procedure.

(1) *Charging Document.* The trial of a misdemeanor may proceed on an indictment, information, or complaint. The trial of a petty offense may also proceed on a citation or violation notice.

**(2)** *Initial Appearance.* At the defendant's initial appearance on a petty offense or other misdemeanor charge, the magistrate judge must inform the defendant of the following:

**(A)** the charge, and the minimum and maximum penalties, including imprisonment, fines, any special assessment under 18 U.S.C. § 3013, and restitution under 18 U.S.C. § 3556;

**(B)** the right to retain counsel;

**(C)** the right to request the appointment of counsel if the defendant is unable to retain counsel—unless the charge is a petty offense for which the appointment of counsel is not required;

**(D)** the defendant's right not to make a statement, and that any statement made may be used against the defendant;

**(E)** the right to trial, judgment, and sentencing before a district judge—unless:

**(i)** the charge is a petty offense; or

**(ii)** the defendant consents to trial, judgment, and sentencing before a magistrate judge;

(**F**) the right to a jury trial before either a magistrate judge or a district judge—unless the charge is a petty offense;

(**G**) any right to a preliminary hearing under Rule 5.1, and the general circumstances, if any, under which the defendant may secure pretrial release; and

(**H**) that a defendant who is not a United States citizen may request that an attorney for the government or a federal law enforcement official notify a consular officer from the defendant's country of nationality that the defendant has been arrested—but that even without the defendant's request, a treaty or other international agreement may require consular notification.

(3) *Arraignment.*

(**A**) *Plea Before a Magistrate Judge.* A magistrate judge may take the defendant's plea in a petty offense case. In every other misdemeanor case, a magistrate judge may take the plea only if the defendant consents either in writing or on the record to be tried before a magistrate judge and specifically waives trial before a district judge. The defendant may plead not guilty, guilty, or (with the consent of the magistrate judge) nolo contendere.

**(B)** *Failure to Consent.* Except in a petty offense case, the magistrate judge must order a defendant who does not consent to trial before a magistrate judge to appear before a district judge for further proceedings.

**(c) Additional Procedures in Certain Petty Offense Cases.** The following procedures also apply in a case involving a petty offense for which no sentence of imprisonment will be imposed:

**(1)** *Guilty or Nolo Contendere Plea.* The court must not accept a guilty or nolo contendere plea unless satisfied that the defendant understands the nature of the charge and the maximum possible penalty.

**(2)** *Waiving Venue.*

**(A)** *Conditions of Waiving Venue.* If a defendant is arrested, held, or present in a district different from the one where the indictment, information, complaint, citation, or violation notice is pending, the defendant may state in writing a desire to plead guilty or nolo contendere; to waive venue and trial in the district where the proceeding is pending; and to consent to the court's disposing of the case in the district where the defendant was arrested, is held, or is present.

(B) *Effect of Waiving Venue.* Unless the defendant later pleads not guilty, the prosecution will proceed in the district where the defendant was arrested, is held, or is present. The district clerk must notify the clerk in the original district of the defendant's waiver of venue. The defendant's statement of a desire to plead guilty or nolo contendere is not admissible against the defendant.

(3) *Sentencing.* The court must give the defendant an opportunity to be heard in mitigation and then proceed immediately to sentencing. The court may, however, postpone sentencing to allow the probation service to investigate or to permit either party to submit additional information.

(4) *Notice of a Right to Appeal.* After imposing sentence in a case tried on a not-guilty plea, the court must advise the defendant of a right to appeal the conviction and of any right to appeal the sentence. If the defendant was convicted on a plea of guilty or nolo contendere, the court must advise the defendant of any right to appeal the sentence.

(d) **Paying a Fixed Sum in Lieu of Appearance.**

(1) *In General.* If the court has a local rule governing forfeiture of collateral, the court may

accept a fixed-sum payment in lieu of the defendant's appearance and end the case, but the fixed sum may not exceed the maximum fine allowed by law.

**(2)** *Notice to Appear.* If the defendant fails to pay a fixed sum, request a hearing, or appear in response to a citation or violation notice, the district clerk or a magistrate judge may issue a notice for the defendant to appear before the court on a date certain. The notice may give the defendant an additional opportunity to pay a fixed sum in lieu of appearance. The district clerk must serve the notice on the defendant by mailing a copy to the defendant's last known address.

**(3)** *Summons or Warrant.* Upon an indictment, or upon a showing by one of the other charging documents specified in Rule 58(b)(1) of probable cause to believe that an offense has been committed and that the defendant has committed it, the court may issue an arrest warrant or, if no warrant is requested by an attorney for the government, a summons. The showing of probable cause must be made under oath or under penalty of perjury, but the affiant need not appear before the court. If the defendant fails to appear before the court in response to a summons, the court may summarily issue a warrant for the defendant's arrest.

**(e) Recording the Proceedings.** The court must record any proceedings under this rule by using a court reporter or a suitable recording device.

**(f) New Trial.** Rule 33 applies to a motion for a new trial.

**(g) Appeal.**

**(1)** *From a District Judge's Order or Judgment.* The Federal Rules of Appellate Procedure govern an appeal from a district judge's order or a judgment of conviction or sentence.

**(2)** *From a Magistrate Judge's Order or Judgment.*

**(A)** *Interlocutory Appeal.* Either party may appeal an order of a magistrate judge to a district judge within 14 days of its entry if a district judge's order could similarly be appealed. The party appealing must file a notice with the clerk specifying the order being appealed and must serve a copy on the adverse party.

**(B)** *Appeal from a Conviction or Sentence.* A defendant may appeal a magistrate judge's judgment of conviction or sentence to a district judge within 14 days of its entry. To appeal, the defendant must file a notice with the clerk specifying the judgment being appealed and must serve a copy on an attorney for the government.

**(C)** *Record.* The record consists of the original papers and exhibits in the case; any transcript, tape, or other recording of the proceedings; and a certified copy of the docket entries. For purposes of the appeal, a copy of the record of the proceedings must be made available to a defendant who establishes by affidavit an inability to pay or give security for the record. The Director of the Administrative Office of the United States Courts must pay for those copies.

**(D)** *Scope of Appeal.* The defendant is not entitled to a trial de novo by a district judge. The scope of the appeal is the same as in an appeal to the court of appeals from a judgment entered by a district judge.

**(3)** *Stay of Execution and Release Pending Appeal.* Rule 38 applies to a stay of a judgment of conviction or sentence. The court may release the defendant pending appeal under the law relating to release pending appeal from a district court to a court of appeals.

# Rule 59.  Matters Before a Magistrate Judge

(a) **Nondispositive Matters.** A district judge may refer to a magistrate judge for determination any matter that does not dispose of a charge or defense. The magistrate judge must promptly conduct the required proceedings and, when appropriate, enter on the record an oral or written order stating the determination. A party may serve and file objections to the order within 14 days after being served with a copy of a written order or after the oral order is stated on the record, or at some other time the court sets. The district judge must consider timely objections and modify or set aside any part of the order that is contrary to law or clearly erroneous. Failure to object in accordance with this rule waives a party's right to review.

(b) **Dispositive Matters.**

(1) *Referral to a Magistrate Judge.* A district judge may refer to a magistrate judge for recommendation a defendant's motion to dismiss or quash an indictment or information, a motion to suppress evidence, or any matter that may dispose of a charge or defense. The magistrate judge must promptly conduct the required proceedings. A record must be made of any evidentiary proceeding and of any other proceeding if

the magistrate judge considers it necessary. The magistrate judge must enter on the record a recommendation for disposing of the matter, including any proposed findings of fact. The clerk must immediately serve copies on all parties.

**(2)** *Objections to Findings and Recommendations.* Within 14 days after being served with a copy of the recommended disposition, or at some other time the court sets, a party may serve and file specific written objections to the proposed findings and recommendations. Unless the district judge directs otherwise, the objecting party must promptly arrange for transcribing the record, or whatever portions of it the parties agree to or the magistrate judge considers sufficient. Failure to object in accordance with this rule waives a party's right to review.

**(3)** *De Novo Review of Recommendations.* The district judge must consider de novo any objection to the magistrate judge's recommendation. The district judge may accept, reject, or modify the recommendation, receive further evidence, or resubmit the matter to the magistrate judge with instructions.

## Rule 60.  Victim's Rights

(a) In General.

(1) *Notice of a Proceeding.* The government must use its best efforts to give the victim reasonable, accurate, and timely notice of any public court proceeding involving the crime.

(2) *Attending the Proceeding.* The court must not exclude a victim from a public court proceeding involving the crime, unless the court determines by clear and convincing evidence that the victim's testimony would be materially altered if the victim heard other testimony at that proceeding. In determining whether to exclude a victim, the court must make every effort to permit the fullest attendance possible by the victim and must consider reasonable alternatives to exclusion. The reasons for any exclusion must be clearly stated on the record.

(3) *Right to Be Heard on Release, a Plea, or Sentencing.* The court must permit a victim to be reasonably heard at any public proceeding in the district court concerning release, plea, or sentencing involving the crime.

(b) **Enforcement and Limitations.**

(1) *Time for Deciding a Motion.* The court must promptly decide any motion asserting a victim's rights described in these rules.

(2) *Who May Assert the Rights.* A victim's rights described in these rules may be asserted by the

victim, the victim's lawful representative, the attorney for the government, or any other person as authorized by 18 U.S.C. § 3771(d) and (e).

(3) *Multiple Victims.* If the court finds that the number of victims makes it impracticable to accord all of them their rights described in these rules, the court must fashion a reasonable procedure that gives effect to these rights without unduly complicating or prolonging the proceedings.

(4) *Where Rights May Be Asserted.* A victim's rights described in these rules must be asserted in the district where a defendant is being prosecuted for the crime.

(5) *Limitations on Relief.* A victim may move to reopen a plea or sentence only if:

**(A)** the victim asked to be heard before or during the proceeding at issue, and the request was denied;

**(B)** the victim petitions the court of appeals for a writ of mandamus within 10 days after the denial, and the writ is granted; and

**(C)** in the case of a plea, the accused has not pleaded to the highest offense charged.

(6) *No New Trial.* A failure to afford a victim any right described in these rules is not grounds for a new trial.

## Rule 61.   Title

These rules may be known and cited as the Federal Rules of Criminal Procedure.